I CAN START OVER

Torn Curtain Publishing
Wellington, New Zealand
www.torncurtainpublishing.com

© Copyright 2023 Syprina Quiroz. All rights reserved.

ISBN Softcover 978-0-6457827-7-6
ISBN EPub 978-0-6457827-8-3

No portion of this book may be reproduced, stored in a retrieval system or transmitted in any form or by any means—electronic, mechanical, photocopy, recording or otherwise—except for brief quotations in printed reviews or promotion, without prior written permission from the author.

Unless otherwise noted, all scripture is taken from the Christian Standard Bible®, Copyright © 2017 by Holman Bible Publishers. Used by permission. Christian Standard Bible® and CSB® are federally registered trademarks of Holman Bible Publishers.

Scripture quotations marked NLT are taken from the Holy Bible, New Living Translation, copyright © 1996, 2004, 2015 by Tyndale House Foundation. Used by permission of Tyndale House Publishers, Inc., Carol Stream, Illinois 60188. All rights reserved.

Scripture quotations marked MSG are taken from THE MESSAGE, copyright © 1993, 2002, 2018 by Eugene H. Peterson. Used by permission of NavPress. All rights reserved. Represented by Tyndale House Publishers, a Division of Tyndale House Ministries.

Scripture quotations marked KJV are taken from The Authorized (King James) Version. Rights in the Authorized Version in the United Kingdom are vested in the Crown. Reproduced by permission of the Crown's patentee, Cambridge University Press.

Scripture quotations marked TPT are from The Passion Translation®. Copyright © 2017, 2018 by Passion & Fire Ministries, Inc. Used by permission. All rights reserved. ThePassionTranslation.com.

Typeset in Adobe Caslon Pro, Azo Sans, League Spartan

Cataloging in Publishing Data
  Title: I Can Start Over
  Author: Syprina Quiroz
  Subjects: Christian living; Personal testimony; Addiction; Trauma and healing; Prison; Rehabilitation; Spiritual growth; Memoir; Biography.

I CAN START OVER

Syprina Quiroz

To my sweet angel baby, Levi.

I'm always thinking of you. I will remember you always and love you forever.

and

To Marlon, Ellah, and Leo.

Thank you all for being a huge part of my life. You are the pieces that God continues to gather together in my life to make His big picture come to pass. You've given me the space to grow, and continue to grow.

CONTENTS

Author's Note		1
Chapter 1	Losing Everything	5
Chapter 2	The Downward Spiral	21
Chapter 3	Encountering Jesus	35
Chapter 4	Facing the Consequences	45
Chapter 5	Mission Trip to Arkansas	57
Chapter 6	Surviving Rehabilitation	69
Chapter 7	Life on the Outside	81
Chapter 8	The Road to Wholeness	93
Chapter 9	Saying Goodbye to Fear	105
Chapter 10	A Transformed Life	115
Acknowledgments		121
About the Author		123

AUTHOR'S NOTE

It was clear where my life was heading. I was on a dark, destructive path, and the lie I had been living had finally caught up with me. I could no longer deny the pain that daily gripped my heart, nor did I want to. Yet from this place of brokenness, when I was at my very worst, God rescued me. In my darkest hour, He forgave me, redeemed me, healed me, and set me free. In one day, I went from believing I was completely hopeless to having hope in Christ.

This is my story.

My purpose in writing this book is to encourage you that this hope is available to you, too. If your story is anything like mine, you've had to walk through a lot of difficult times. Perhaps even now you are grieving a tragic loss, battling an addiction, or struggling in your faith. Whatever your circumstances may be, I want you to know you are not alone and we are on this journey together.

I have experienced a lot of dysfunction in my life yet I now see that those difficult times were defining moments that led me to Jesus. The trials are still ongoing—even since accepting Jesus as my Savior I have suffered from anger, depression, demonic oppression, identity loss and suicidal thoughts. I have learned, however, to walk in the confidence of knowing that I am a new person whose identity is secure in Christ alone. The hardships and pain that I've experienced have been constantly molding and shaping me into the person I am today, and they have taught me that God will never leave me or forsake me (Deuteronomy 31:6). He is with me—always!

Today I am continuing to grow in my knowledge and love of God. His is the only opinion that truly matters; He alone holds the rights to my life. In Him I have found a freedom I could never have imagined. It's not simply a testimony of my life being transformed from despair and darkness into a great and glorious light—He is the very reason I am alive today. Every day I wake up and breathe, and every day I choose Him.

The process of beginning again has required my complete surrender to God—a consistent, daily decision to deny myself and instead choose to trust God in *every* circumstance. I have spent many hours at the altar in the presence of God asking Him to change the way I think about myself and to help me entrust my own desires and dreams to His sovereign will. In doing so, I have received the unfathomable gifts of His healing, His love, and His grace.

I want you to know that though it may be difficult to begin again, it is possible with Christ. Whatever you may believe about yourself, you are not disqualified because of your past. You are not worthless. If you allow God's truth to penetrate your heart, God can rewrite your story and turn it into something beautiful! It doesn't matter what your past may look like or the mistakes you have made. I want you to know you are *called* by God. He has a plan and purpose for your life! And it is all for His glory!

AUTHOR'S NOTE

In the book of Isaiah, God gives us this hope:

> To all who mourn in Israel, he will give a crown of beauty for ashes, a joyous blessing instead of mourning, festive praise instead of despair. In their righteousness, they will be like great oaks that the LORD has planted for his own glory.
>
> **Isaiah 61:3, NLT**

It is no coincidence that you are here, and I believe you are reading this book for a purpose. It is my sincere prayer that through opening my heart and sharing my story, you too will find healing and hope in the dark places, and your heart and life will be fully transformed through the work God wants to do in your life.

CHAPTER ONE

LOSING EVERYTHING

I was twenty years old when I lost my mom. I still remember every detail as if it was yesterday. At the time, we didn't know how serious it was. She thought it was just a cold, and it didn't even cross our minds that it could be anything more. She was taken into hospital the day after Christmas having been sick for a couple of weeks, and she passed away within a week of being admitted.

The day I got the news that changed me forever, I was with my two sisters. My stepdad, who had been with my mom the entire week she was in the hospital, suggested we gather together, and on the way to meet them I felt a deep sense of dread. *God, please don't let her be gone*, I prayed over and over. It was a desperate cry of hope, even though, somehow, I knew it was already too late.

Once we had all arrived at my sister's house, my grandpa put my stepdad on speakerphone. I could hear the brokenness and devastation in his voice as he murmured, "Girls . . . she's gone!" All at once, we lost it, falling to the ground as though our hearts were literally sinking from the shock. I simply couldn't believe what was happening. In that moment, I knew I had to call my biological father. We didn't have a particularly strong relationship, but within the past couple of years we had been closer than we had been for a decade. I knew he would want to know about my mom, and that he would try to be there for me as I embarked on this journey of grief.

When my mom died, a piece of my soul died with her. I no longer felt whole. *How would life ever feel normal anymore after such a tragic loss?* I used to call my mom every single day after work. We became close after high school when I moved out to live with my boyfriend. I enjoyed hearing her complain to me about all the crazy things happening at home, reminding her on those occasions when she would share too much, "I'm not your friend remember, I'm your daughter!" It's true what they say: You never truly realize the impact a person has in your life until they are gone.

Initially, all I could do after receiving the devastating news was weep and weep to the point of numbness. The hardest part of it all was having a little brother who couldn't understand why his mom wasn't there anymore. I feel his pain even now, because, unlike me and my sisters, he never got to experience what it was like having Mom be there for him growing up.

Grief gave my life a whole new outlook. I didn't know if there was a 'right way' to grieve, and there were times I didn't even recognize it because it took on so many different forms. Sometimes the pain would escalate suddenly, resurfacing old wounds hidden deep in my heart. Other times, sadness and depression snuck up on me like a ninja when I least expected it—like the time I smelled the scent of the candle Mom always bought when I was in a store one day, and found myself reliving old memories of our time together.

When Mom died, I wasn't following Jesus, and my faith was pretty much non-existent. I was living the way *I* wanted to live and trying to fill myself with the world's empty offerings. I'd prayed in the car for God to save my mom's life, but was I really a believer? I didn't really know the difference. I may have grown up in church and heard the Word of God from a young age, but I certainly didn't have a personal relationship with Jesus. I had already experienced so much suffering in my short life, and I truly didn't even know if God *could* heal such brokenness—or if I even wanted Him to.

∼

From a very young age I had been led to believe that what other people thought about me was the truth. I allowed my worth to be dictated by others—by the way they treated me. I had a difficult time in the school I attended while living with my mom. I was very shy and didn't like to be the center of attention. Whenever I was, it was usually only because other kids were making fun of me.

One time, a friend told me she wouldn't be allowed to go to my house because we lived in a trailer. I also remember that one school picture day, when I was six or seven years old, I wanted to wear a dress and the heels my mom had found for me at a thrift store. I was all dressed up with curls in my hair, and I felt so pretty walking down the hallway . . . until I heard, "Those shoes are so ugly. Why would you wear shoes from a thrift store?" These silly, childish remarks have stayed with me long into adulthood, heightening every single insecurity.

I had crooked teeth and an overbite before I had braces. I was never embarrassed about smiling until someone mocked me, pushing their front teeth way forward while I was laughing one day in middle school. I can't tell you how many times I was picked last or laughed at during gym class because of how I looked or my lack of athletic ability. These early childhood experiences had a dramatic impact on my self-esteem. It was as if I had a target on my back. I felt like I had no purpose and would never achieve anything or be good enough for anyone.

Boys had never liked me or even noticed my existence unless it was to tell me I was out during a dodgeball game. It was a surprise, therefore, when I found myself suddenly getting noticed by guys in high school. When it came to dating, sometimes I would say yes, no matter how unsuitable they were, just because I felt bad. I had experienced a traumatic event when I was very young that distorted the value of saving myself for marriage. I was yet to understand my true worth. Perhaps that is why, for many years, I felt incapable of choosing—or waiting for—the right one.

I was convinced as I got older that love meant being affectionate and giving myself away to others. Subsequently, I became clingy and emotionally dependent upon others. When I started dating my boyfriend at fifteen, we soon became physically intimate with one another. My sense of worth was defined by what *he* thought or believed about me. But after two years of being together in high school, we broke up, and I was heartbroken. He was the first boy I had ever 'loved', and I had given a precious part of myself away to him. Now, I was really convinced I was worth nothing. *If he didn't love me, no one would love me.* I felt so alone and became severely depressed. I had never experienced this feeling before, and I didn't think I would make it through to the other side.

Around this time, I vividly remember taking a picture of myself in the hallway of our trailer and thinking, *All I want is for someone to love me. I want a husband. I want to be able to get married, to have a beautiful gown, and live happily ever after.* In that same moment, however, I believed I would never be someone's first choice to love. My self-esteem had plummeted and the rejection I felt from the recent breakup was devastating.

A short time afterward, I found out my ex-boyfriend was dating someone else. *Ugh!* A friend called and told me the news, then invited me to a party that night so I "would forget about all of my problems." She made a rule that every time his name was mentioned I had to take a shot of alcohol. Although I had never actually had a drink before then, I was swayed by her sly way of helping me 'drown my sorrows'. That night, I opened the door, at the tender age of seventeen, to healing my pain with alcohol. The night did not end well for me.

Unaware of how strong a hangover could be, I still went to church the next day. It happened to be the Sunday where the youth led the choir, and we all sat on benches in front of the entire congregation. I wanted to throw up every time I opened my mouth to sing and attempted to hide behind the hymnbook. A girl pulled me aside and told me how inappropriate my behavior was. I told her I didn't know what she was talking about, but like most people who knew me and how I behaved at school, she didn't buy it. I certainly wasn't the only girl going to parties, drinking, or flirting with guys, and usually it was the guys who approached me, but because I also went to church, I was the one who was blasted and ridiculed for my behavior. It was as though I was the only one to blame.

By the time I had reached my senior year, I had a bad reputation and was regularly being called horrible names by my peers. Broken and without an outlet or a place to heal, I was unable to decipher what was best for me. I had reached a place where I just didn't care. My misplaced attempts to manage the pain on my own had backfired, resulting in poor decisions I couldn't take back.

One high note during this time was connecting with a friend who was in my oral communications class. I was always so nervous when I had to speak in front of people, but he noticed me and encouraged me that I had done a good job. I didn't know his history, but I had heard he had a drug problem and had been working hard to overcome it. He didn't want to disappoint anyone anymore, and he had started giving speeches in class about the negative effects of doing drugs and how to change your life. He was also a great basketball player and a favorite of our school principal.

We became good friends, and I began calling him after school. I even invited him to church with me on a Wednesday night—and when he came, he told me he liked it. The next day he didn't come to school, and I had a feeling something was wrong. When I called to check on him, I heard from his brother that he had been caught with drugs again and wasn't doing well. The following Friday morning, he died by suicide.

My friend's death happened two days before my birthday, and his funeral ended up falling on the day I had planned my party. I had an invitation for him. Though he was going through some issues, he was a really kind person, and I liked him a lot. I typically didn't open up to anyone close to me about how I was feeling, and I'm not sure if I even knew how to express what was going on inside my head.

When the senior class was sent home from school on the day we were given the news, my mom and stepdad sat me on the couch to ask me if I was okay and if there was anything they could do. At that time, it was difficult for me to share anything personal with my mom, perhaps because of the separation between us when I was younger. I had wanted to be with her, but instead I spent most of my time with my dad in another state. Even though she never gave me a reason not to, it was such a struggle to trust her with my problems. We didn't have that kind of relationship, but only because *I* didn't want it.

After my friend's passing, things only got worse. My ex-boyfriend's new girlfriend was the one who had been constantly calling me names and making fun of me, and seeing him with her caused me so much pain that I truly wanted to end my life. The battle within my soul had become desperate. One day I wrote him a note telling him how much I loved him and that if he didn't want me, I didn't want to live. He shared the note with some close male friends of mine, and agreeing I needed help, they immediately walked me to the counselor's office. They knew what I wrote couldn't be ignored and worried that if they didn't act, the same thing that happened to our classmate could happen to me.

My mom was shocked when the counselor called her to come and pick me up. She even seemed angry, perhaps because she had tried so hard to understand me, but I still wouldn't share anything with her. I knew she cared so much about me, but I still couldn't open up.

Though I didn't end my life, I would still cry myself to sleep at night wondering if there was any purpose for me. I was so lonely; I didn't have a date for the prom, and it seemed like no one wanted to be with me. I cried out to God and asked Him to send me someone who would love me. The hatred I had for myself was so strong. I didn't like the way I looked, and the criticism I had heard since childhood rang in my ears every time I looked in the mirror. I know now that a solid relationship with my father would have made all the difference, but at the time, I had no idea. I started to get very self-conscious about my weight, to the point of becoming bulimic. I had been in cheerleading for four years in high school, but when senior year came and the season ended, the lack of physical activity resulted in weight gain.

I was academically challenged throughout high school, maybe because of everything that was going on in my life, and I hadn't sought help besides having a counselor come into the school to speak with me periodically. I couldn't tell if it helped me or not. Still, I managed to graduate with a C average—a D in my algebra class, and Cs in my math and history classes. I was eighteen years old by this time and couldn't wait to graduate.

When I moved away for college, I was ready for a fresh start. I didn't think I needed my parents; I thought I could do it on my own. Yet my longed-for freedom lasted only a week! I had intended on staying in a dorm room with one of my close friends, but she made other plans instead. My new roommate was not a good fit and being at college was nothing like I thought it would be. Truthfully, I wasn't mature enough to handle moving away, and I missed my mom so much. The feeling was mutual—according to my sister and stepdad, my mom cried all the way home after dropping me off at college. So, a week later, I moved back home. I got a job at a fast-food restaurant and enrolled myself in the local college close by.

A few weeks later, I met my new boyfriend. Despite not knowing one another very well, our relationship escalated quickly. I'm not sure if you would call it attraction or lust, but it was definitely not love. Nevertheless, I fell for him so quickly that I was blind to any red flags. Soon, I moved in with him and his family. On occasion, we would drive to my parents' house, and he would get high in the car on the way there. Eventually, I adopted that lifestyle too, and over time, my destructive behavior intensified.

Not only was I getting high every weekend, but I would also drink to excess. It got to the point where I was even going to work high on marijuana. I knew it was wrong, but I decided to risk it anyway. *He was doing it, so why shouldn't I?* I reasoned. I'll admit it seemed fun for a while; I felt as though I didn't have a care in the world, and I was numb to the realization that what I was doing was hurting me. However, as this lifestyle continued, my mindset began to shift. Never in my life had I been around so many people high on drugs or drunk. I felt anxious and overwhelmed every time I walked into a party. I didn't know how they could live this way. I realized I had become a different person, and it was someone I didn't want to be. It was only my desire to be in a relationship that kept me in this pattern of behavior. All I wanted was to be loved.

The constant drinking and partying weren't enough to fix the pain I felt at losing my mom, but I didn't know how else to navigate life with grief. I was hurting and broken, but continuing this destructive lifestyle and being in a relationship felt stupid and pointless now that my mom had passed away. By this point, however, my anxiety and depression had increased, and I sought comfort anywhere I could because I didn't know what else to do. I was about to learn that when we cling to other things instead of the only One who can center us and heal us, they can ultimately end up destroying us.

～

A year after losing my mom, I was finally moving forward with my life and starting to feel optimistic about my future. I started a new job in a pawn shop which paid more and would provide an opportunity for me to break free from the sea of credit card debt I was currently swimming in. By this point, I had accrued quite a few credit cards but had stopped making payments when Mom died. I was already so overwhelmed that it felt easier to just ignore it rather than reach out for help. Still, I was hopeful I could get out of the mess I had created for myself, and I could finally feel a sense of my old self coming back.

My relationship, however, was not in a good place. My boyfriend was reluctant to change his behavior, and we started fighting a lot. I had trouble sleeping because of my anxiety and the nightmares I'd been having since losing Mom, and I eventually became addicted to over-the-counter sleep-aids. It got to the point where I was taking up to six pills per night because I was so desperate for rest. Then, my three-year relationship finally ended, and everything fell apart. The rejection took me down a dark, self-destructive path, and this time it was even worse than before.

I was furious the night we broke up. I couldn't understand why this was happening after I was starting to feel better about myself and my life. I wanted him to understand what I was going through, but instead of comprehending or having compassion, he walked away. Angry and embarrassed, I ended up taking a shot of alcohol and driving away from him and all his friends at the party we were attending. I was so hurt and broken that I didn't even think about what I was doing. I just drove. As I was driving, however, my vision became distorted until I could barely see the clock on the dash. Realizing my rash decision could have severe consequences, I stopped myself in time and returned to the party until it was safe for me to drive home.

~

It's frightening to think how much I despised myself in that moment. Blinded by rejection and pain, my life continued on a trajectory of self-destruction. Truthfully, I also wanted revenge on my boyfriend, yet no matter what I did, none of my negative behavior appeared to affect him. I have since learned that a spirit of unforgiveness only hurts the one choosing not to let the hurt go. I thought I was making a difference by holding onto it, but ultimately, I was only hurting myself.

As humans, we are prone to repeatedly having the same reactions to hurtful situations. The cycle will repeat itself until we invite the Holy Spirit to touch the wounded places in our soul, enabling us to walk in freedom. When I became a Christian and began a relationship with my now-husband, I knew I needed healing from the repeated hurts I had experienced. Every time I felt rejected, I blew up. The pain was so deep. When I said yes to Jesus, I wanted to break the emotionally destructive patterns I had grown up with; I wanted to have a legacy through Christ and live righteously. *Inviting Him in* was the key to overcoming the self-loathing I had lived with for most of my life. And, if you have endured your own seasons of self-hatred or feelings of worthlessness, it might be a key step in your healing journey, too.

With Christ, you *can* be set free from this kind of pain. No matter how you feel about yourself, starting over is possible. In fact, "nothing will be impossible with God" (Luke 1:37). It's never too late for God to do the heart work that is needed. There is no need for shame either. As the Bible says:

> So now there is no condemnation for those who belong to Christ Jesus. And because you belong to him, the power of the life-giving Spirit has freed you from the power of sin that leads to death.
> **Romans 8:1-2, NLT**

Even after becoming a Christian, I didn't fully understand this. My own desires still bound me and dictated my choices. Yet, if you have ever injured yourself, you know healing is a process. It can be challenging at times, and recovery can take longer than we would have hoped. It's the same when we ask God to heal our hearts; it cannot be rushed. And if I'm being honest, sometimes the wounds we carry or the chains that bind us are not even visible to us. When we can't see it, we aren't aware of it, and when we aren't aware of it, we cannot be free from it.

I have learned that we all carry burdens or trauma from our childhood that we need to bring to the light. The first thing I did when I accepted Jesus was to ask God to take away my drinking problem. Secondly, I wrote out in a journal my testimony of how God saved me.

I then proceeded to acknowledge to Jesus all the sexual relationships I had had in my life. There is a reason the Bible speaks of marriage as a covenant between two people; we weren't designed to give ourselves away repeatedly. Once we receive the Spirit of Christ, the Bible tells us, "Therefore, if anyone is in Christ, he is a new creation; the old has passed away, and see, the new has come!" (2 Corinthians 5:17). However, there is a process that takes place as the Holy Spirit helps us to start over. It took time for me to let go and trust Jesus enough to completely set me free from all that had bound me.

My identity had become wrapped up in the idea of being loved. This is why I had to renounce those relationships. Once I removed those people from life, I had no idea who I was or what my core beliefs and values even were. I'm still learning and growing in the knowledge of who God created me to be. It's a lifelong process, and I still don't know all that God has for me. Yet as I keep walking this road, I know I will continue to be healed, and the process will be worth it. *Jesus* is worth it. This is what God says about us:

> Now this is what the Lord says—the one who created you, Jacob, and the one who formed you, Israel—"Do not fear, for I have redeemed you; I have called you by name; you are mine. When you pass through the waters, I will be with you, and the rivers will not overwhelm you. When you walk through the fire, you will not be scorched, and the flame will not burn you. For I am the Lord your God, the Holy One of Israel, and your Savior. I have given Egypt as a ransom for you, Cush and Seba in your place. Because you are precious in my sight and honored, and I love you, I will give people in exchange for you and nations instead of your life. Do not fear, for I am with you."
> **Isaiah 43:1-5**

When you are faced with the fear of starting over, remember you are never alone. As scary as it may seem, God has already brought you through the 'fire' and the 'deep waters'. He has redeemed you, and He has called you by name. And if you do not know the Lord as your Savior, I invite you to continue this journey with me. There is hope, and He can help you. He can take the old things and turn them into something wonderful and new! No matter how difficult the journey may feel right now, I promise you, it *will* be worth it.

CHAPTER TWO

THE DOWNWARD SPIRAL

After my relationship ended, I had to find another place to live. I moved in with a few friends but ended up getting kicked out because I would spend my money on useless things and didn't pay rent. My drinking became excessive as I tried to numb the pain, and I spent all my money at bars. I was even arrested for public intoxication when the police showed up to my friend's house that was full of underage kids drinking alcohol. I was so incoherent at the time that I apparently fought with the police officer who was trying to get me into the car. (I have no memory of the event.) Thankfully, my sister ended up bailing me out, but it was a dangerous precedent. I was angry and no longer cared about being responsible—my life was spiraling out of control, and I felt powerless to stop it.

By this point, my finances were a disaster. Not only was I overspending, but I was also in significant debt. I continued my pattern of misusing credit cards—when I maxed one out, I would simply add another one, without ever paying them off. I started getting a lot of calls from creditors, but I ignored them. I was reluctant to talk to anyone about my problems.

One friend I was staying with actually ended up taking me to court to pay her what I owed. We were staying in a really nice duplex on a golf course. I had the means to pay for my share of the rent, but I couldn't control my spending. All the money I had earned for rent was wasted on Christmas presents, driving around to meet up with guys, and buying alcohol. Finally, she'd had enough. She needed the rent money, and she informed me she would keep all my belongings until I paid her. After it was settled in court, the judge suggested I get a storage unit for all of my things because I had no other place for them to go. I couldn't afford that, but my ex-boyfriend kindly helped me bring them to my stepdad's house.

The reality of my situation hit me like a ton of bricks when I no longer had my own space or a place to live comfortably. There wasn't another bedroom for me at my stepdad's, so I stayed in the entryway space—a literal 'space' in between the garage and the kitchen. The room fitted only a floor lamp, a small end table and a futon (that I slept on), and it was horribly uncomfortable.

I still had my job, and by this point, I had been promoted to the jewelry counter which I really enjoyed. It didn't take long for me to come up with a solution to help me get out of debt—and my current living situation. I started 'borrowing' cash from the drawer at work. My plan was to take the money, pay my rent, and then return the money when I got paid. I never did. Instead,

I kept stealing and repeating the same cycle every month. As if taking cash wasn't bad enough, I subsequently moved onto stealing jewelry.

It seemed like nothing that I was doing as far as my finances were concerned was working. I had every intention of getting myself out of the rut I was in, but I couldn't figure out how to do it. I just kept digging myself into a deeper hole. One day, when we were closing the store and I was locking away the expensive pieces of jewelry in the safe for the night, a thought struck me. *Take the ring, you can sell it for cash.* Just like that, I put it in my pocket. The adrenaline rush I experienced was incredible, and I was convinced I wouldn't get caught.

The pattern continued. One memorable night, my friends and I took a trip to Springfield to go to a club. I ended up getting really drunk and separated from everyone I knew. Anything could have happened to me as I wandered the streets alone, but my friends had no idea I was even gone. Instead, they'd been giving my phone number out to random people in the club. When we got back home, one of the guys messaged me, and I drove two hours to meet him. I soon made this a habit of mine, stopping at jewelry stores or pawn shops on my way to see him. Each time, I would sit in my car, overwhelmed by anxiety and adrenaline. I had to hype myself up and tell myself that I could do this. I knew I just needed to get rid of all the jewelry I had taken, and everything would be fine.

Eventually, I told myself I would stop at one more pawn shop then I would be done. I wasn't going to do it anymore. The place

I chose was about an hour from home. It had a sign on the wall that read: SMILE, YOU'RE ON CAMERA. Another sign said they would prosecute anyone guilty of theft. As I showed the owner the fourteen-karat gold, heavy rope necklace I had taken from the store, my gut was telling me he was very suspicious. When he asked where I had gotten it from, I made up some story about my stepdad, but I don't think he bought it. I pawned it under my name, with no intention of getting it back. At this point, I thought things couldn't get any worse. I had no idea I was about to lose everything.

～

The day my actions finally caught up with me started like any other. It was a Friday morning, and the pawn shop was deserted. I was at the front of the store waiting for customers while all three of the managers (including my boss) were having a very serious business meeting in the back. One of the managers suggested I leave a few minutes earlier for lunch. I remember going to my car and realizing I had these huge diamond earrings with the little tag still on them sitting in the cup holder. Telling myself I needed to move them in case someone saw them in my car, I ended up hiding them in my wallet inside my purse instead.

After lunch, the pawn shop was much busier. There were a lot of customers in the jewelry section, so I hurriedly put my purse and phone in the cubby before heading over to assist them. Approximately thirty minutes later, I noticed a sheriff come into the pawn shop and wait by the front door. He wasn't wearing a uniform, but he did have a belt with a badge and gun on his side. This wasn't altogether unusual in this line of work as stolen items are often brought into pawn shops in exchange for cash, and we'd recently had a case where someone had pawned a stolen iPod. When the manager started walking over to me and said that the sheriff wanted to ask me something, I automatically assumed it was related to that incident, and I was happy to talk to him.

Soon, however, I realized the sherrif wanted to ask me some questions down at the police station. At this point, I started to get a little suspicious. *Why would I need to go to the police station? And why wasn't his car labelled like a regular police officer or sheriff's car?* Once I hopped into the front seat, he asked me, "Is this the first time you've been taken down to the police station for questioning?" In that moment I froze. Anxiety overwhelmed me, and I could feel the heat coming off my chest as I reached over to strap the seat belt. That's when I understood what was happening. My mind was racing with so many thoughts that I couldn't even begin to answer his question.

When we arrived at the police station, the playing field shifted. The sheriff's whole attitude and demeanor suddenly changed, and I felt deeply uncomfortable. We walked into the building, and I was taken into a small room to wait. In those tortuous minutes alone, I knew this was it! My secret was out, and I couldn't hide any more. Frantic thoughts ran through my mind: *What do I do? There's no way I'm going to get through this. I'm going to have to go to jail, and what if I get locked away for years? Everyone is going to know what I did. I won't have my family or friends to support me* anymore. *I'll have no one!* The only way I could think of to get through this ordeal was by taking my life.

When the sheriff came back into the small holding room, guilt was written all over my face. "Here's the thing," he said as he shuffled some papers around on his desk, ". . . we already know you did something, so you might as well confess now and make this easy. Either way, we have evidence so just tell me how much you took?" Apparently, I had been caught on camera, and my boss had been tracking down the missing jewelry. He asked me to give him a number, but I didn't know. I didn't have time to keep track of all the money, so I gave him a rough estimate of five thousand dollars. "Is there anything else you need to tell us?" he asked. "Do you have anything else in your possession?" Petrified, and hoping my honesty would result in greater leniency, I confessed everything—including that I still had some stolen earrings at my stepdad's house and in my purse at work! *Worst criminal ever.*

I was driven to my stepdad's house to collect the jewelry. He was shocked to say the least. When I handed over the earrings, the officer began to read me my rights. Even worse, my eleven-year-old brother, who was already struggling with the loss of his mom, watched me as I was being arrested. I could see the fear on his face. "It's going to be okay, I promise," I told him repeatedly, but as his big sister—someone who should have been taking care of *him*—I was so disappointed in myself.

My poor stepdad didn't know what to think or do. I asked if he was going to bail me out, and he said it might be a few days before he could come up with something. I panicked. *A few days!* He told me he'd have to sell something or figure it out. I knew he just couldn't believe it, and that this was a big financial burden to place on him. For the first time, the reality of my situation hit me. *I am actually going to jail. I'm going to actually be behind bars, sleeping in a cell, wearing prison clothes.*

This time, I was not politely seated in the front of the police car but handcuffed and put in the back. As we left my stepdad's house, the sheriff called my boss on the phone. "She got caught," I heard him gently say. "Yes, there's evidence." His voice was calm. "We are headed back there now. No, you are not going to do that. I need you to calm down; we're on our way." There were many guns at the pawn shop, and I assumed my boss was wanting to use one of them. I genuinely feared for my life, no joke. I was pretty sure she already despised me because of my past behavior. She had every right to be upset with me. I knew she would be livid.

When we pulled into the pawn shop to pick up the earrings I had hidden in my purse, there were no cars in sight. Everyone had left, and the store had closed early. I saw my boss immediately. This petite woman, leaning up against the countertop with her arms crossed, reminded me of Medusa with snakes coming out of her hair. The anger in her eyes was such that I expected her to turn me to stone or kill me on the spot.

"Are you stupid, Syprina?" she said. "How did you think you were going to get away with this?" I'm not sure why, but I replied, "I thought you were a Christian." She snapped back, "Oh, I *am* a Christian! But I'm going to make sure you pay for what you have done!" She followed me out, and as we were leaving, she told the officer she was going to have my car towed off her property. Luckily my best friend, who lived right around the corner from the pawn shop, said she could pick it up for me. I was so thankful to have the sheriff there with me this whole time, standing up for me, and abiding by the law in the face of my boss' rage. While I certainly do not excuse my actions, it felt to me as though she was being especially cruel. As I was taking my final step off the property, she looked me directly in the eyes and snarled, "I am going to make sure everyone knows who you are and what you have done!" That is exactly what she did.

When I returned to the police station, this time for a theft of property felony charge, someone I knew and had hung out with on numerous occasions booked me in. He couldn't believe it. "You know this is a felony charge, right?" he kept saying. This would be an ongoing theme as my actions came to light. Nobody I knew had any inclination of what I was doing, and most people were in disbelief. I was afraid and begged him not to put me inside with the jailhouse crew. By God's grace, he told me he would do whatever he could to have me stay out on the bench and wait to be bailed out.

After I got my picture taken, and was fingerprinted and booked in, I didn't know who to call. I reached out to my ex—no answer. I tried to call his dad—no answer. I had no idea how I was going to get out. Then, all of a sudden, I was told someone had posted my bail! It was my ex-boyfriend's mom's ex-boyfriend. Try saying that three times! I couldn't believe it. We met at the bondsman's office afterward, and I told him I would get him his money back *somehow*. After selling my brand-new iPhone I was able to pay him back. He had always been kind to me, and we'd had several conversations when I was living with my ex about my life and how hard it was for me losing my mom. I knew he had a heart for me, and he knew I wasn't a bad person but advised me to do whatever I could to get some money because my old boss was going to come after me. He said she knew a lot of people, and on top of that, she was in the Chamber of Commerce, so she had a lot of people on her side. He wished me good luck, and said he hoped the best for me.

My best friend cared deeply for me, and she had been there for me through my rollercoaster ride of emotions. When I went to pick up my car from her, she told me how betrayed she felt. She couldn't understand why I hadn't just asked her for help or money if I'd needed it. It was hard to explain. I had wanted to tell people, but I didn't know how. *How could I tell even my best friend all the things I was doing? Surely, she would have judged me.* Still, it turned out I had lost her anyway. "I don't even know you anymore," she told me. Sadly, this event would mark the end of our friendship. I was heartbroken. I wasn't looking for someone to overlook my actions; I was looking for someone who might understand.

∼

The day after my arrest, I woke to the reality of my consequences. There was a heaviness on my chest that felt like a literal elephant was sitting on it; I couldn't breathe! I had no idea what to do next. I reached out to another close friend who asked me if I had a lawyer. There was no way I could pay for a lawyer; I had no money saved, I just lost my job, and I was in debt. She told me to fill out an application for a public defender who could represent me in court. She also advised me that there would be another court date and a trial. Hearing these details made the desperation of my situation painfully clear. It must have been difficult for everyone in my life to process. Nevertheless, from the depth of the pit I was in, Jesus was drawing me. I could feel it; I just didn't know it yet.

That morning, I started listening to rap music like I usually did while getting ready. When the music started, however, it just felt wrong! I wanted to eliminate everything I was doing that might provoke any sort of bad behavior. Music was one of those things. I stood in the bathroom and tried to remember any Christian song that I could put into my music station. It took a long time. I had not listened to Christian music in years. Then, it came to me: *How Great Is Our God*. The band had played this song at church camp when I was around sixteen years old, and I remembered liking the lyrics.

Then, a second thought came to me as I got ready: *Where's my Bible? I need to read my Bible!* I had a purple Bible in my room though I hadn't read it since I was a little girl. I dusted it off and started reading the book of Matthew in the New Testament. I didn't know what I was reading, and I was really upset that I couldn't understand what God was saying to me. Still, I was so convicted that I wept. I wanted to make this a part of my life. I realized if I opened the Bible and read it, even if I didn't understand it fully, I would find the truth about the right way to live. I just knew

Jesus would forgive me if I asked Him, and even if no one else would, He would. In that moment I began praying, crying out to God in desperation and asking Him to forgive me for what I had done. I was facing a mountain of consequences, and I was petrified. But after praying to God, I felt peace. At this point in my life, I hadn't been to church in several years, but suddenly I knew, *I gotta go to church!* There was just no stopping me. There was a church down the road from where I lived, and on this particular Wednesday night, I decided to go.

I was unbelievably uncomfortable. There were about ten people sitting in the pews, and they were all older than I was. All I wanted to do was cry. I tried so hard not to completely break down, because I didn't want them all staring at me. *Surely, they knew that I didn't attend church there, and I was the youngest person in the sanctuary?* Despite my discomfort, I was so convicted as the Word of God was preached that I could not sit still.

The message that night was on the topic of heaven. The pastor spoke about the streets of gold described in Scripture, and how Jesus has prepared a mansion in heaven for those who believe in Him. He talked about what a glorious day it would be to finally reach eternity and walk on those golden streets. We would no longer have sorrow or experience any pain, and we would be completely set free! My heart broke. I needed heaven. I needed hope.

After the service was over, I approached the pastor and asked if I could speak to him. He sat me down on the bench by the front door. I needed to confess, so I gave him a brief overview of what had happened. I said I was scared, and I wasn't sure what to do next. Then he told me I needed to turn myself in. I realized he probably thought I was running from the law, not that I had already been caught! *Great, a pastor thinks I'm a fugitive! Could this get any worse?* I asked if he could be praying for me, and he reassured me he would. I left feeling a little lighter from all the heaviness I was carrying.

Confessing my sins to Christ first and then making them known to the pastor that day is what first invited me into the presence of God. I began to seek Him earnestly. I needed to know more. I needed to find Jesus. He was the only One who could make things right for me and reconcile me to Himself.

I couldn't see it at that moment, but after I became a Christian, God took me back through all these hopeless moments that led to my arrest. He showed me that even in those times of loneliness, He was right there in the room with me. There was one particular moment before my arrest when I was sitting on my couch in despair. I was desperate for help but couldn't talk to anyone about what was going on. Yet the Lord was waiting for me to come to Him, standing in the room with His arms open wide. He wanted to help me, but I couldn't see Him.

There are many times in our lives when we feel such grief and despair and think, *Where is God? Why would He let me go through this?* But the truth is, He is right there beside us, waiting for us to come to Him. Jesus is a gentleman, so He won't be forceful with His presence. But there are many grace moments where He gently nudges us or puts a thought in our minds. This is Him drawing us into His arms.

The Bible clearly shows us how much Jesus cared for His disciples, and even when it looked like He was leaving them, He wanted them to grasp hold of this truth, "I will not leave you as orphans [comfortless, bereaved, and helpless]; I will come [back] to you" (John 14:18 AMP). In the same way, we can trust that Jesus truly knows us and cares about every aspect of our lives. Look at these words from King David:

> Before a word is on my tongue, you know all about it, Lord . . . Your eyes saw me when I was formless; all my days were written in your book and planned before a single one of them began. God, how precious your thoughts are to me; how vast their sum is! If I counted them, they would outnumber the grains of sand; when I wake up, I am still with you.
> **Psalm 139:4,16-18**

What can I do? Where do I go? Who can I ask for help? A lot of these questions can paralyze us from moving forward. Believe me, I know. Our circumstances can become so overwhelming at times. Rest assured that no matter what you might be walking through or how heavy your personal burden may feel, God has never left your side. He knows you intimately, and He continues to draw you to Himself. There is no secret that can be hidden from God (Psalm 139:11-12), and there is no condemnation for those who are in Christ Jesus (Romans 8:1).

It doesn't matter how far you may have fallen or what you may have done; I encourage you, like I did, to confess and lay the burdens you are carrying at His feet. His light can shine into the darkest of places, and His love can reach to the depths of our despair. In Him alone can we finally receive forgiveness and experience true freedom.

CHAPTER THREE

ENCOUNTERING JESUS

After I confessed my need for Jesus, He continued to draw me deeper into the plans and purposes *He* had for me. But it wasn't a one-sided relationship. I continued to read the Bible to ground myself in the truth and prepared my heart and mind to obey His Word by spending regular time in prayer. At that time, I didn't have a plan, but I was trusting God in each moment. I knew I was forgiven, and there was a deep sense of peace that came with that, even though I wasn't sure where I was headed.

My old boss was following through with what she said she would do. She tracked down all my friends and family members, wanting to know everything I was doing and who I was hanging out with so she could use it against me. Finally, my stepdad told her it was time to leave me alone, that I deeply regretted my behavior and had even gone back to church. She didn't want to hear it. She continued to badmouth me and tried to turn every person I knew against me. *And for what?* I was already paying the price for my actions, and it still wasn't over. Yet, in spite of all this I kept telling myself, *I'm forgiven. Jesus already forgave me.* I still felt guilty, but it motivated me to keep taking one more step in the right direction. Hope was not lost.

Have you ever felt so shameful you wanted to hide? That was me. I wouldn't even go to the store until after dark, for fear of running into someone I knew. The desire to move away was constant. I didn't see a future there, and I had to figure out a plan. *But how?* I had no money, and I didn't know where I could work at this point. I decided to sell as much as I could—my clothes, shoes, TV, DVDs, CDs, you name it. My sister lived in town, so we attempted a yard sale at her house to try and find a way to begin again somehow. Things were going very well with the yard sale; I had over two hundred dollars! Then someone stole the cash box.

That's what happens when you steal, I thought. *God is punishing me, and this is what I deserve.* I was devastated. It was all that I had, and I was trying to make things right. Sitting in my sister's living room, I didn't know what to do. I decided to call Bill, my biological father. I didn't know if there was any way he could help me, but I felt he needed to know what was going on anyway, and I'd rather he heard it from me first. I told him I was in trouble. I was facing charges, and I wasn't sure what was going to happen. "I am disappointed in your actions," he told me, "but I'm not disappointed in you." I'm not sure if he knew the impact of his kindness to me in that moment when I felt so awful. I was so grateful for his support.

He asked me if I wanted to come and stay with him for a couple of days at least—maybe even go to church with him. I didn't know it, but he had been asking the church to pray for me before he even knew what was happening. He truly cared about me, and he didn't want me to live a life of hell—or worse, end up there. So, I went.

~

The thought of leaving town to stay with my dad felt like a new beginning. *Could this be my answer?* I wondered. *Is God giving me another chance?* As I drove to his house with my sister, a month after I had been arrested, I had no idea what to expect. My dad had told his church I was coming to visit, and the very next night, we went to a Wednesday night meeting. It felt far less intimidating than my most recent visit to church.

The pastor invited people to come up to the altar area at the front to worship. They had their hands lifted and were praising God. Though I was looking around trying to take in everything and observe what was going on, I could feel God's presence drawing me closer. I felt the same spirit of conviction as I did when I sat in the pew of the small Baptist church back home, only this time there was a peace that I hadn't experienced before. Eventually, I simply couldn't handle sitting in my seat anymore—I had to go to the front! I thought my sister, who had traveled more than four hours to come to church with me, was going to go up with me, but she hesitated. It didn't stop me though. It was a step of faith in the right direction. I was overcome with emotion, and I was scared because I was in front of everyone. Though I was seeking a life with Jesus, the consequences I was facing weighed heavy on me. It was hard not to wonder if people knew my story or what they thought of me. *Did they know? Could they tell?*

Jesus was in that church building, and the love I felt in the room was so strong. The presence of God in that moment filled me with hope and helped me overcome my anxious thoughts. I felt total peace—something I had not experienced since I was a little girl in the Pentecostal church. Yet whatever it was, I wanted more of it. I looked up and saw one of our lead pastors. Tears were flowing from his eyes as he was worshiping, and it was as though the Lord was wanting me to see something I hadn't before. I knew that he genuinely loved Jesus, and as I stood there, I said to myself, *Whatever it is that he has, that's what I want.*

While I was in the service that night, I knew there was nowhere else I wanted to be. *I had to keep coming to this church.* I felt so much love that night. They didn't judge me. It was the answer I had been searching for; I just didn't know the *how*. I had no money and there were still debts I needed to pay. I no longer had a job, and truthfully, I didn't want to live with my dad because there was still a lot of mending that needed to be done. Still, God had opened a door for me, and I knew it was the only way forward. I talked to my dad and told him I wanted to stay and to keep coming to the church. "Alright," he told me, "we will figure it out."

When I returned home to tell my family about my decision, some were not impressed. I was described as 'selfish' and 'such a brat'. Yet, I knew moving away and going to that particular church was the only way to get the help that I needed. There was no life for me back home. My family couldn't help me, and finding a job in such a small town would have been nearly impossible. Honestly, I thought my old boss would find out where I worked and get me fired—that's how angry she was. The only person in my family who encouraged me to leave was my stepdad. Looking me in the eyes, he told me he supported my decision, and if this was what I needed to do to feel better, then I had to go. He knew that I was seeking God for answers, and it was a positive step in the right direction. The date I would be leaving was July third—his birthday. Yet, he reassured me that he loved me, and he could never be angry at me.

I knew it was hard on all of them—the month of July was such a family-oriented month with so many birthdays to celebrate and my mom and stepdad's wedding anniversary. It was also our tradition on the fourth of July to gather together and watch the fireworks as a family. The night I left, I sat in my car talking to my little brother. It felt like God orchestrated that moment between us even down to the fireworks popping in the background. I knew it would be hard for him, and maybe he even thought he was losing me, too. He was going through a lot, and I didn't want to leave him, but I had to do what was best—for both of us. I knew he was watching me, and without our mom around, I wanted him to have an older sister he could look up to. As heartbreaking as it was for him, I knew it was the right decision. It was already really late to start the four-and-a-half-hour drive, but I drove like a speed demon and held my bladder. I couldn't get there fast enough to start my new life!

Two weeks after moving in with my dad, I got a job! A woman from my childhood church worked at a temp agency and found a company that would hire people with a criminal record. I couldn't believe it! I had called my pastor and told him I had a job opportunity, and he prayed that God would honor my attempts to seek Him and show me favor. When I was offered the position, I felt so blessed—especially as my dad had been unemployed for the past eleven months and money was tight. I would start my job within a week.

The Sunday before I began working at my new job, my dad and I visited a church in the same district as ours, where one of the guys my dad had mentored was preaching. That night, the message was about how big our God is, bigger than all the stars in the sky and galaxies in space. I was blown away. You may have never had the chance to see the night sky in the country, but it's beautiful. In my hometown, the sky was so big and clear at night, and I used to sit in awe and wonder at the beauty of the stars. I felt a tug on my heart and connected so tangibly with the message that there is a God who is big enough to help me overcome. I had always been drawn to nature and it felt as though the Lord was drawing me to Himself.

That night, I made my commitment official. There was an altar call and those who wanted to rededicate themselves to the Lord were invited to come to the front and receive prayer. A group of us went up, and I said yes to Jesus! I was surrendering my life fully to Him—and this time, I meant it. I remember standing at the altar touching the cross necklace I had happened to put on that morning, *knowing* that now I was different. It was the day I gave my heart to Jesus, and I will never forget it.

Encountering Jesus was a completely different experience for me. I had always gone to church and said I believed in God because that's what the Bible tells us to do. But now I had fallen in love with being in the presence of God. It is an experience of heaven on earth, and it forever changes you. I told myself I didn't want to drink anymore or be drawn by the lusts of the world, and I asked God to take these things away and help me to live righteously. I thought these things would satisfy me but instead, they had ended up consuming me. It can happen to us all. Even when our lifestyle seems so satisfying in the moment, we don't realize the long-term consequences: addiction, debt, bankruptcy, divorce, even suicide. I didn't want to live that way anymore; I knew it was wrong. What I wanted was more of Jesus. God's presence satisfied me more than anything else ever could, and once I was aware of it, I didn't want to ever escape it.

∼

When God draws us to Himself, He helps us see what needs to change. Sometimes there's so much clutter in our lives, we do not even know *how* to move forward. For me, one of my biggest struggles was not having any money and not having the slightest clue how to overcome the mountain of debt I had put myself in. However, if you are a son or daughter of the Highest King, you can trust He will guide you along the path that will ultimately make things right. Each situation is going to be different, and while some are more difficult than others, God wants to grab us by the hand and carry us through.

You might be wondering: *What are the steps? How can I start over? How can I get the help I need?* One of the first steps is to make a call. Sharing can be liberating, and it can also bring healing. Reaching out to the right person or finding the right connection can enable you to keep going as you seek to follow God and His path of righteousness.

It was my dad's and my church's prayers that led me to surrender my life to Christ. But I wasn't finished yet. Our walk with Christ is expected to progress. If we quit in the middle of the storm or trial, how can we experience the full extent of His unfathomable love for us? We can't. I have seen many people who were reluctant to believe in what Christ had for them. They walked away in the middle of their mess without being deeply healed. They missed knowing and understanding the true love that's found in Christ. Only in Him can we truly understand who we were made to be—a new creation, wholly loved by our Father in heaven. Those I have known were drawn away because of the pain of their life circumstances. But God is greater than any pain or tragedy, and by rejecting Him, they missed out on the fullness of what He had for them.

Experiencing the forgiveness of Christ is what brought me true life change. He died on the cross for me—and for each one of us. He did what we couldn't do for ourselves, and He bore every painful moment on our behalf. This unfathomable act of love brings us healing, freedom, joy, and peace. It's beyond addiction, beyond betrayal, beyond divorce, beyond rejection, beyond debt, and beyond our most shameful moments.

As Paul writes in Ephesians 2:4-6:

> "But God is so rich in mercy, and he loved us so much, that even though we were dead because of our sins, he gave us life when he raised Christ from the dead. (It is only by God's grace that you have been saved!) For he raised us from the dead along with Christ and seated us with him in the heavenly realms because we are united with Christ Jesus" (NLT).

My slate had been wiped clean. Everything that I had done up until that moment was forgiven. In the Psalm 103:12 (NLT) we read, "He has removed our sins as far from us as the east is from the west." My once-scarlet sins were as white as snow (Isaiah 1:18).

Our response to this abundant forgiveness should be one of repentance. When we repent, we are saying no to sin and yes to Christ's life within us. This is how we move forward and prevent ourselves from being bound by anything that would keep us from the things of God.

Look at this verse from the book of Hebrews:

> "Make sure that no one falls short of the grace of God and that no root of bitterness springs up, causing trouble and defiling many. And make sure that there isn't any immoral or irreverent person like Esau, who sold his birthright in exchange for a single meal. For you know that later, when he wanted to inherit

the blessing, he was rejected, even though he sought it with tears, because he didn't find any opportunity for repentance."
Hebrews 12:15-17

Our repentance is instrumental in our ability to inherit God's blessing and experience the fullness of life we have in Him. It is a change of mind that recognizes the error and consequences of our sins and embraces the grace we have in Christ to begin again with a clean slate as we walk in His forgiveness and love.

It's important to be aware of where you might currently be struggling. Then, make it known to Christ. Once you say yes to Him and offer genuine repentance for your past mistakes, He doesn't separate Himself from you, *ever*. If you are concerned about something, He is concerned with you. If there is a hidden area you know you are struggling with, seek council. If your heart is genuine, it may be that God is exposing the sin and wants you to be set free from it.

True freedom can only be found within the Spirit of God—and it is never too late. Who would have thought that right when I messed up as badly as I possibly could, Jesus would say, "Now is the time to draw her to myself!" Friend, He can clean up any mess, He can restore any home, He can recover any addict, He can heal any bitterness and contempt. He can even fix finances! I want you to know I believe in you. God is rooting for you, and He will until the very end. There is nothing too hard for our God!

CHAPTER FOUR

FACING THE CONSEQUENCES

For a year, I had been serving the Lord fervently. I was a new believer, but God had truly changed my heart and life and I was eager to keep moving forward in my walk with the Lord. In spite of this transformation in my spiritual life, however, I could not escape the consequences of my past.

My probation had begun, and it forced me to embrace a whole new level of humility. There are different forms of probation depending on the severity of your punishment, and I had to check in with my parole officer every two weeks. If I missed my appointment, I could get deported back to Arkansas, be given another court date, or serve time in jail. Prior to my first visit I was petrified, but I knew I had to follow through. As far as the officer is concerned, you're there because you committed a crime, and that is all they know about you. When my officer followed me into the bathroom to pee in a cup while she watched, I was so angry and embarrassed! I wasn't doing any drugs, and I wasn't the same person I was before. That, however, was irrelevant in the eyes of the justice system.

After a few visits, I was fortunate enough to transfer my probation to the town I worked in. I worried about running into someone I worked with, but it was more important for me to maintain my job. I had worked hard to earn a permanent position, and I was sending as much money as I could to my public defender to show that I was taking the consequences seriously and working hard toward paying off restitution. Above all, I desperately didn't want to go to jail!

I knew God had given me this chance to start over with Him, and I wanted to do whatever I had to do to make it right. I would get up every day at the crack of dawn to work in the warehouse while still trying to be a light to others and figuring out how to have a relationship with my dad. It wasn't easy. Then my dad finally found a job, and I had to drive him to work early in the mornings before driving to work myself. One morning after dropping him off, I looked down at my phone to play some music, and the next thing I knew I was slamming on my brakes due to an incident up ahead. I not only hit the car in front of me, but I was also hit from behind. My car was totaled, and, even worse, I did not have insurance.

The consequences of my brief moment of inattention were significant. I was now without a car (with little hope of getting a new one due to a poor credit report) and my license was suspended. On top of that, I was required to pay the coverage for the two vehicles I hit with my car, which ended up totaling almost eleven thousand dollars! It seemed overwhelming on top of the debts I had already accumulated—especially since my old boss had now reported sixty-five thousand dollars worth of jewelry stolen from the pawn shop! It seemed a suspiciously high figure, but there wasn't much I could do. At this point, it seemed nearly impossible for me to pay all my debts—not including probation fees, public defender fees, and now three added payments relating to the accident. Thankfully, my pastor knew a lawyer who got involved in my case and was able to convince the judge to change the violation on my record to a lesser, non-moving violation. Praise God for His favor!

My dad ended up taking me to and from work for a year. The tension of it all overwhelmed me, and there was conflict in our relationship. I didn't know what to do except cry out to God for a vehicle. I had no idea how this would ever be possible, but I kept on praying. When I received a little over a thousand dollars from my tax refund, I wanted to put it toward a new car, but my dad really thought I should send all of it to the public defender in Arkansas. After continuing this process, and faithfully trying to pay off my debts in spite of my ongoing car difficulties, I genuinely thought God would clear my criminal record so I could move forward with my life in Him.

There were two Scriptures I memorized during this time. One was from Hebrews 11:1:

> "Now faith is the substance of things hoped for, the evidence of things not seen" (KJV).

The second was from Jeremiah 29:11:

> "For I know the plans I have for you," says the Lord. "They are plans for good and not disaster, to give you a future and a hope" (NLT).

It sounded promising. I was being faithful, and in return, I envisioned that God was going to wipe the slate clean. Unfortunately, that wasn't what happened.

∼

By this point, I was anxiously awaiting my trial date. I had received a couple of continuances, and the trial had ended up being pushed back for a year. That year gave me precious time to prepare myself for what awaited me. I was facing serious charges, and I was scared. Yet God was indeed working behind the scenes on my behalf to 'give me a future and a hope'— I just didn't know it.

One way He did this was through my friendship with Hurley. He was eighty years old when I met him at work on a day when I was particularly agitated. It was summertime, and the warehouse where we built garage doors had no air conditioning. I was battling with one of the women about using the fan. When I left to go on my break, she would turn it off, and when she left for her break, I would turn it back on. No matter what we did, we just couldn't get along. Another lady was yelling at me because I was apparently banging the metal slats too loudly, and when I started singing worship songs quietly to myself, she told me to be quiet.

FACING THE CONSEQUENCES

When I was asked to go and help in another department with even fewer fans, it all became too much for me. I was already hot and bad tempered, so I threw a fit right there at work. Immediately I caught myself and thought, *There's no way I am setting a good example as a Christian.* I recognized my behavior was unacceptable and wasn't representing Jesus well.

All of a sudden, this older gentleman came over to talk to me. He had worked there for a long time, and he was a Christian, too. He loved people and would always talk to them about the Lord. "You look like someone who serves the Lord Jesus Christ!" he said to me. I was shocked by his words, but the Lord had laid it on his heart to talk to me and build a strong friendship. It was the beginning of a beautiful relationship.

Given my previous experience with men, at first, I thought it was strange for him to invite me to eat with him and then pay for my meal. *What was it that he was drawn to about me?* He sat in the booth across from me as we were eating our food and talked to me about Jesus. He told me his wife Betty had passed away several years ago. When he talked about her, his face would light up. I knew he loved her so much and couldn't wait to meet her again. When she died, he moved in with the only son he had left out of three boys. He had already 'retired' from the warehouse job a long time ago but needed something to keep him busy, so he came back. I'm so grateful he did!

To think that this godly man from Iowa moved to the Kansas City area and was working at *my* warehouse—the first job I had as I started my life over—*only God!* I didn't think of myself as a good Christian, but the way he treated me (which was how a kind and gentle father would treat his child) helped me to understand that I wasn't the same person I was before. It may have felt easier to throw in the towel and return to the world's ways, but he reminded me that I had a new identity in Christ, and I needed to persevere in my walk with Him.

God knew what He was doing placing Hurley in my life at this exact time. Even now, I could never imagine my life without him—he poured so much love out on me that it broke through the hard, fallow ground of my heart so I could love in a way I hadn't before. Christ purposely put him in my life because He knew I needed someone to love me. And I would certainly need his prayers and encouragement for what was awaiting me in the coming season.

~

I returned to Arkansas. It was August 23rd, 2012, the day of my sentencing. I will never forget it. The night before, I was staying with my sister and I was so petrified I was shaking, but I remember sitting on the couch praying, "God, you know that I love you and I want to live my life for you. You know I won't be going back to my old life, so I pray that you would clear my record and take everything away. In Jesus' name, amen."

I hadn't experienced it before, but while praying, it felt as though those weren't the right words to pray. The reason was, God already knew the outcome. I was trying to pray for *my* will to be done, and it certainly wasn't in His plan to take it all away.

The trial itself was a brutal experience. I was sitting next to my public defender, Andrew, the whole time, but some details are a blur to me. I remember that the owner of the store was still passionately angry, as she had every right to be, and wanted me to receive the worst punishment possible. When she testified, she tried to say that I stole sixty-five thousand dollars worth of jewelry but was quickly corrected by my public defender and the figure was changed to sixteen thousand dollars instead. There was no way I pocketed anything even close to that amount either, however, they had to consider the market value of the jewelry that had been stolen. She wanted me to have at least five years of jail time and probation and to pay back every dollar I had stolen from her.

While it was still a frightening experience, I genuinely believe the Lord had His hand on me. I thank God I had people on my side who were praying for me and representing me in the court room. The prosecuting attorney was very loose with his words and accusations, but over in Missouri my godmother was praying that the Lord would hold his tongue if he were to say anything vile. She also prayed God would give me favor with him and with the judge. My lead pastor even testified on my behalf. Despite the prosecuting attorney's attempts to manipulate the responses, she answered calmly and truthfully. She wanted to let them know I was genuinely changed.

Andrew also fought hard for me. This was another sign of God's favor. He was amazed when he saw me again after a year and even said, "You look different!" When the court dismissed for a break, he told me, "It looks like you will have to serve some time, but I'm going to push hard for probation instead of five years in prison." *Five years!* I couldn't believe it. He told me that if I shared my story and explained to the judge what I had been doing this past year, he might be able to reduce my sentencing by quite a bit. Still, he wasn't certain. He didn't know the judge very well and felt that he may be difficult to negotiate with. He wanted to prepare me, however, that no matter what we did, I would likely have to serve some jail time.

When the court was back in session, I was the last person to speak. Just before I took the stand, I prayed this verse from Matthew 10:18:

> "You will stand trial before governors and kings because you are my followers. But this will be your opportunity to tell the rulers and other unbelievers about me" (NLT).

Then, I asked Jesus if He would grant me favor with man and with God. When I went up to read my letter, I looked directly at the judge who was listening intently to everything I was saying. I apologized publicly for my actions and conveyed my remorse for what I had done. I also made them aware that I had found Christ and would be lost without Him in my life. When I sat down, I was shaking. The only thing left to do was wait for the verdict.

I didn't have to wait long. The judge said that five years of prison time was not very reasonable at all and recommended my boss think about forgiving me and moving on. Still, I was ordered to spend a hundred and twenty days at a women's recovery facility, followed by ten years of probation. I was required to pay all the court fees leading up to this point, as well as the sixteen thousand dollars (in monthly payments of two hundred and fifty dollars) after serving my sentencing at the facility. I would be placed in the county jail until a bed opened up at the recovery center, and after going home to say goodbye to friends and family, I had to turn myself in first thing Monday morning. Court was then adjourned!

Andrew told me to be grateful I was allowed to return home as this was not the norm, and urged me to make sure I was here, no matter what, the following Monday. He also told me to eat my favorite food before turning myself in because I would be without it for the next four months! I told him I was going to eat some fried chicken, and then we left.

Driving home with my dad, the reality of the verdict hit me. I started to panic, and I didn't know what to think. I was so grateful for all the prayers and support, but ten years was an extremely long time to endure probation. From my understanding, they had to extend it because of the amount of restitution I would have to pay, but it still felt overwhelming. The decision was final, however. There was no going back.

My dad encouraged me to be grateful that God had His hand over the entire court session especially since the prosecuting attorney had pressed hard for me to serve five years in prison. He reminded me that even though I had to face the consequences of my actions, I still had Jesus. I had given my life to Him, and

I meant it. He was working in all things for my good and His glory—even if it didn't necessarily feel like it.

~

God could have taken away all my charges like I wanted Him to, but He didn't. You see, God bore the suffering of the cross because He knew we would have to go through trials. He died to clear our record of sin, but also to demonstrate that we can have victory through our seasons of suffering, because we have Jesus to cling to. As Jesus awaited His crucifixion in the garden, He was in such anguish that blood streamed down His face as He prayed: "My Father, if it is possible, let this cup pass from me. Yet not as I will, but as you will" (Matthew 26:39). He hadn't even committed a crime, but God didn't spare Him from the cross.

Sometimes we can be confused about the trials we encounter as Christians. Jesus knew He had to endure the cross so we could receive salvation. He didn't make any promises that we wouldn't suffer after becoming a Christian. Instead, Jesus gave us hope that through the cross, we could overcome anything!

> "For the joy that lay before him, he endured the cross, despising the shame, and sat down at the right hand of the throne of God."
> **Hebrews 12:2**

A trial may also be a form of discipline coming from a place of love from our heavenly Father. We read in Hebrews 12:5-6: "My son, do not take the Lord's discipline lightly or lose heart when you are reproved by him, for the Lord disciplines the one he loves and punishes every son he receives."

In His kindness, this is what Christ has done for me. When I say the process isn't easy, believe me, it isn't. Yet, it's always worth it.

> "No discipline seems enjoyable at the time, but painful. Later on, however, it yields the peaceful fruit of righteousness to those who have been trained by it. Therefore, strengthen your tired hands and weakened knees, and make straight paths for your feet, so that what is lame may not be dislocated but healed instead."
>
> **Hebrews 12:11-13**

As believers, we are called to be faithful in the face of trials. Hebrews chapter eleven is known as the 'faith chapter' because it shares a testimonial of the trials and victories of great leaders of faith who have gone before us. They give us a biblical standard to move forward in faith, even though they never received their promise this side of heaven. Because of the desire to know the Father's heart, God created them to be warriors. He produced in them courage, strength, wisdom, and honor. He used the thing that had them feeling defeated, and turned it around for His good.

It's an important reminder that God often has a bigger plan for our life than we could ever possibly imagine—and sometimes that means we have to face difficult times to draw us closer to Him. Be encouraged that no matter how hard things might seem, He will give you the strength and endurance you need to overcome any situation as you walk in the hope of the promise to come.

CHAPTER FIVE

MISSION TRIP TO ARKANSAS

The Sunday before I reported to jail, I was a nervous wreck. I didn't know what to think. *Would I lose my salvation? Would I still be a Christian after all of this?* Fear was an understatement, but I clung to the promise that God pours out His blessings on those who love Him and others. As we read in Proverbs 11:25:

> "Those who live to bless others will have blessings heaped upon them, and the one who pours out his life to pour out blessings will be saturated with favor" (TPT).

At church that morning, God gave me a word through my pastor. "Syprina," she said, "I know this may seem like a severe punishment, but God is telling me this is a mission trip to Arkansas! God has been preparing you for this, and He will use you in a mighty way for His good! He is sending you there, and He's going to use you. He says not to be afraid but to trust Him in the process!" As I was about to embark on one of the most incredibly humiliating experiences of my life, that word spoken over my life gave me much-needed hope that God was not going to leave me to face it alone. He was pouring out a covenant of kindness on me as He did for King David in Isaiah 55, and He was giving me a promise in the process. The enemy sought a punishment, but God was determined to turn my life around for my good! He was committed to making my paths straight.

After returning to Arkansas to serve my time, I met up with my stepdad to say goodbye. He was worried about me and didn't know how I would be able to go through with it. I could see the look of concern on his face, and he was angry that he couldn't be there for me like I needed him to be. It would have been too hard for him to even see me in jail. "Don't worry," I told him. "God is mightier than any person or any force that would try to come against me! He is a big God, and He is bigger than what I'm about to face." I had no idea how my own words would later minister to him when he faced his own trials.

When I reported to the county jail, they took my fingerprints and a 'mugshot' of me. I then had to change into a black and white jumpsuit in front of a female police officer. She proceeded to do a full scan of my body from head to toe to make sure I wasn't smuggling anything in; it was horrific! I was being treated like a criminal and the lack of privacy in particular felt utterly humiliating. I wanted to keep my body private, but I no longer had a choice.

I was adamant about bringing my Bible into jail with me. Books were the only possessions we could take with us, and I knew God's

Word would be the one thing that would hold me together while I was in there. Before I left, I had also asked my friends and family to write their addresses and phone numbers in the front and back pages so I could send them postcards. I knew I would have a lot of downtime. As I was getting booked in, the officer examined my Bible and asked if I was going to smoke the pages. "What? What does that even mean?" I replied. The officer told me that inmates would regularly tear out pages and smoke them, and he wanted to make sure I wouldn't be using it for anything like that. "No!" I responded, more than a little shocked. I had never even heard of such a thing. "I brought my Bible in so I could read it." My jail education had evidently begun.

All eyes were on me—the 'newcomer'—as I walked into a room full of women, carrying only my Bible and a mat to sleep on. *"Okay, Lord, here we go,"* I whispered quietly under my breath. I felt so intimidated and fearful. Almost immediately, I had to decide who I wanted to share a room with. Some women invited me to room with them, but the thought of sharing my space with so many others overwhelmed me. I ended up finding a smaller room, though it did mean sharing with someone who didn't practice good hygiene. Even though I have a weak stomach, I decided to stay where I was. I appreciated the extra privacy, and I knew that if I wanted to represent Christ and minister to the 'least of them' (Matthew 25:40), I would have to make some sacrifices along the way.

After speaking to many of the women there, I realized they had been in and out of jail for a long time. They could quickly see that I was different, and knew I hadn't had much experience getting in trouble. All I wanted to do was hide in my bunk, which I did as soon as I laid my mat down on the cold metal bed. I was completely out of my comfort zone in this unfamiliar territory, though I was thankful when a couple of women came and introduced themselves to me, which helped me feel more at ease.

It was a small facility compared to most. Our living area was a large open space with gray walls that extended to high ceilings. Metal tables and chairs were fixed to concrete floors and there were two staircases on either side. The rooms were on two different levels, and at that time, they were mostly full. Each room had the capacity to bunk four people. They had plexiglass windows and a half concrete wall to enable you to at least use the bathroom in privacy, away from the prying eyes of the officers and fellow inmates.

At night, the doors were automatically locked at a certain time and weren't opened until breakfast the next day, and all the lights besides the main lights were turned off. There were nightly walk-throughs where an officer would shine her flashlight into every room to make sure we were abiding by the rules, specifically relating to contraband. These were illegal items that were brought into the jail or those that had been transformed into something that was dangerous.

We were served breakfast, lunch, and dinner at almost the exact same time every day. There were a lot of 'Peter Pan' moments where we imagined there was an extravagant feast before us, but unfortunately, the real food never lived up to our expectations.

For example, for breakfast we would have plain oatmeal and black coffee. Once a month, we would get biscuits and gravy. Lunch was a bologna sandwich (no cheese), plain rippled chips, a small chocolate chip cookie, and lemonade. For dinner we would have baked beans with green onion, cornbread, mixed vegetables, and sweet tea. I soon learned to save my cornbread for a snack to have later when I got hungry!

There was no television, no payphones, and no radios, so we did nothing all day except converse with each other, eat, and go to bed. If the weather was acceptable, we would be allowed to go outside as a group for about thirty minutes. The outside area was a small concrete square with a high fence. There was far more space to walk inside, and it was easy to get some sort of exercise by doing laps around the sitting area. We could have a visitor once a week and receive postcards in the mail. All the postcards had to be read and screened, however, before we were even able to receive them.

I was mortified to discover there was only one shower between all us women. *One!* It had a curtain-like covering for privacy, but it was right next to a door that was frequently used by the officers. If they needed to walk through that door while someone was showering, they would see everything. One time I was showering, and a jailer came in with a couple of women shuffling behind him. *Lord Jesus, help me!* The thought of anyone seeing me when I showered triggered significant anxiety. I realized all the things I'd taken for granted. Even now, I'm still grateful when I use a public bathroom and there's a door to protect my privacy.

I learned from a wise woman at church to use conditioner for my dry skin, since there was no lotion available. Every time I stepped into the shower; I prayed that the blood of Jesus would cover me—I was a germophobe, and it was difficult sharing the shower with so many women who had been on and off the streets. Many had drug problems, and there was a high probability they had been exposed to diseases like hepatitis. There's no telling what kind of life people have lived before coming to jail.

The hardest part of my journey was not having a support system when I needed someone to turn to, when I didn't know what to do, or when I felt lonely. Yet God knew exactly what I was going to need! I know that He led me to my church so that I would have community while in jail. Each week I received postcards from friends there who gave me such encouragement. Their love and support enabled me to feel like I was a part of the body of Christ, even though I wasn't able to attend physically. Our spirits were connected through Christ. These letters also served as a powerful testimony for the women in the facility with me who saw the love and support I was receiving from my church every week.

On my birthday week I received twenty postcards! Even the youth group from my church sent me an encouraging note. God knew exactly what I needed at all times and gave me the right words from a specific person each week to encourage and strengthen my faith. He was faithful in delivering what He said He would do to get me through this. I don't know if my church family realized it at the time, but the guards were reading each postcard they sent too, including Scripture verses or testimonies. What a great ministry opportunity! I also became a witness to Christ for the women serving time with me who were, perhaps for the first time, able to see what it looks like when you surrender your life to God. It felt like I was truly on mission for God.

∼

We spent a lot of days playing games of *Spades* to pass the time, and I got really good at it. I earned the nickname 'Gospel Gangster' because I could play a mean game of cards, and they thought I was an angel God had sent to help them. There were so many heartbreaking stories, and I grieved for these women who didn't know Jesus. I knew He desired for them to be healed and set free just as I had been.

One woman talked strangely for her age. She was quite a character, but substance abuse had affected her skin, and she had dark spots on her face. She was very popular with the other women, and I really didn't want to be on her bad side.

I met another girl in jail who was the same age as me, and she was pregnant. Her head would twitch when she spoke, and when she walked, she would fling her arms. I had never seen anything like it. She later told me it was due to a meth withdrawal. She loved the baby's father and wanted to be a good mom and take care of her baby, but her drug use kept leading her down a dark path.

A few girls who I had gone to school with ended up in jail at the same time as me. One of them particularly intimidated me. She had always been very aggressive and wasn't afraid to start fights. Another woman (who had always been one of the popular kids and had participated in several beauty pageants as a teenager) smuggled substances in for the others to smoke, which may seem like a needless risk to take, but addiction is a big part of the lives of men and women who are in and out of jail. For me, alcohol had been the substance of choice. It altered the way I thought, and it led me to the consequences I was now facing.

Amazingly, the Lord was able to use me in the lives of all those women. One woman shared how she was feeling very depressed; she was scared about what might happen when she was released. I brought my Bible in and laid it on her bed for her to read. I had it open at Psalm 139. Tears were streaming down her face as she told me it was exactly what she needed to read, and it had touched her deeply.

Another night I noticed the same woman in a cell downstairs by herself and felt led to go in and start talking to her. She shared with me that some other inmates were plotting something against her, and she was a bit afraid. This is one of the most significant ways Jesus used me in the facility because the women trusted me enough to share details of their lives. Stepping into a jail cell forced us all to accept the reality that what we did was wrong, and we all felt guilt in various forms. We didn't get to see our families; we didn't have any luxuries—everything was stripped away. All we had was time to think about how we ended up in this place, and I was fortunate to be able to use that time to be a light to others.

Later, we had a 'pow-wow' in one of the girl's cells. With tear-filled eyes, one woman shared how angry she was at that inmate for snitching on her drug dealer and ruining his life, and how she wanted to punish her. "I had it all planned out," she said to me, with a hint of humor. "Then you walked over to us with your sweet little smile and angel face. When you walked into the cell with her, I knew I couldn't do anything because you were in there." I was so thankful that God had used me in that situation, and that I had followed His leading.

That night, the conversations between the women in the room got deeper and more intense. One woman shared about the first time she started using, and how she got caught. One described what it was like to watch her two children be taken away. Another confided that she got into the habit of shoplifting because her addiction had taken away all her money. It was such a significant conversation. I was honored to be a part of these women's lives and to be trusted with their stories, but my heart burned with grief. They didn't have what I had found in Christ. They were lost and broken and hurting, and their lack of hope resulted in them repeating the same cycle of destructive behavior over and over again.

After our 'pow-wow' that night, a fellow inmate asked if I would pray for her. She would typically hear voices and laugh or talk out loud when no one else was around. We went into another room, and I prayed over her before going our separate ways. The next day she told me that something about her was different since I prayed for her. She would sing quietly to herself. I had a few moments alone with her outside, and I started singing, *This Little Light of Mine*. She had a huge smile on her face, but there was a part of the song that she couldn't sing: "Don't let Satan blow it out." I knew she was bound by demons, but I told her Jesus had authority over the devil, and He has the final say over everything. She was still afraid, so I prayed for her again, that she would believe and trust God for victory over the dark things in her life.

Then there was an older woman who came into the facility. I could tell by her demeanor that life was weighing on her. She had been in federal prison before and been on suicide watch at times. She had a beautiful voice and would often sing to herself. One day she asked if I liked to sing too, and if I would perhaps sing something for her. I was too shy to just sing right there and then, but she asked if I could learn a song she had heard on the Christian radio station. She wrote down the lyrics and gave them to me. I knew this was an opportunity for the women to experience Jesus, so I prayed He would anoint me, and when I sang, the song would bring healing and show them the hope of Christ.

The day I sang for them was actually my birthday. I had been in a bit of a funk because since my mom died, my birthday made me feel depressed. Mom would always do whatever she could to make me feel special because I have always been a little 'extra' when it comes to my birthday! However, these sweet women threw me a surprise party. They used their commissary to make me a cake (which was a big deal!) and one of them even made roses from toilet paper. I had no clue how she did it, but they were so pretty. I was so honored that they would go out of their way to do so much for me to celebrate my birthday.

While they were in the room, the older woman asked if I would go ahead and sing. I took a deep breath and told her I would have to close my eyes because I was so scared. In that moment, it felt like a bucket of hot anointing oil was poured over me from heaven—it was so hot I started to sweat. I knew it was a God-moment. When I was finished, I opened my eyes and saw tears streaming down the older woman's face and in the eyes of other women. She said my song touched her heart deeply, and again I was so honored that God could use me even *here*.

CHAPTER SIX

SURVIVING REHABILITATION

I ended up spending half of my sentence in the county jail and the second half in a state 'rehabilitation' center. I was dreading the transition, and when the news came that I would be leaving jail, I started to panic. I remember one woman coming into my room to 'encourage' me, but it was not the affirmation I was hoping for. She told me not to worry—she was sure it would be nothing compared to federal prison where violence always broke out, women got raped, and inmates had to sleep with one eye open.

Now more than ever, God's Word became my lifeline. Gathering all the prayers I had written, postcards from my church family, and Scriptures that I had taped to the bed frame of my bunk, I clung to His promises. 1 Peter 1:6-7 became especially precious to me:

> "So be truly glad. There is a wonderful joy ahead, even though you must endure many trials for a little while. These trials will show that your faith is genuine. It is being tested as fire tests

and purifies gold—though your faith is far more precious than mere gold. So when your faith remains strong through many trials, it will bring you much praise and glory and honor on the day when Christ is revealed to the whole world." (NLT)

I spent Thanksgiving that year in county jail before being transferred to the rehab center. A local church donated a special meal for the inmates. It was the best food I had tasted in weeks. It was also a tangible reminder of God's care—a reminder I would need more than ever in the days to come.

~

Thankfully, my close friend was being sent to the rehabilitation facility at the same time as me. Bottles of shampoo and conditioner were a hot commodity in jail, and as I packed my belongings, I knew I wanted to give mine to the lady I had been bunking with. I wanted her to know that she was especially loved, even though the only thing I had to give her was my mediocre offering of shampoo and conditioner.

I placed my humble box of possessions in the trunk of the police car, and my friend and I finally left around ten o'clock that morning, ready to embark on this unfamiliar next chapter. On the way, the police officers who were driving us decided to stop at McDonald's for coffee, and to our surprise they brought us back breakfast burritos and orange juice. We were in awe. Nothing had ever tasted sweeter! Quietly to myself, I gave thanks to God in the back seat of the car for the blessings He had poured out on me up to that point.

But that was just the start. The drive took about four hours, and for the whole trip we listened to country music on the radio. When a particular song came on, it felt as though the Lord was ministering directly to me through the lyrics. I knew then that He was still with me, and that even though I didn't know what lay ahead, I was going to be okay, and I would be back home in no time.

The state rehabilitation facility was drastically different from anything I'd experienced before. The intake process began as soon as we arrived, and it was mortifying—it involved showering, applying lice shampoo to the top of our heads and changing into new clothes with officers watching us the entire time. We also had no idea where they had put our things, which was very disorienting. We then had to leave a urine sample in a cup for drug testing and complete a psychiatric test. After that we were held in a tiny room for a couple of days while we waited for a bed to be assigned. There were about twenty or thirty women in our intake, and although there were perhaps five hundred women in the facility, each of us was assigned to a different dormitory.

The campus itself was large, with a barbed wire fence surrounding the buildings to prevent us from escaping. The 'rehabilitation center' was more of a disciplinary facility. Our daily routine was strict, and included classes, groups, chapel, and chores. Every morning we were woken at 4:30 a.m. and we had to make our beds, military-style. There was even someone assigned to check each bed was made correctly before we were allowed to leave for breakfast.

Our attire consisted of a long-sleeved, pale-yellow shirt and pants. When we stood, we were instructed to place our hands behind our backs, and we were expected to respond to those in authority with, "yes, ma'am," and "yes, sir." If any rules were broken, we would get 'written up'. Too many write-ups could result in another charge being added to our criminal record, so we quickly learned how important it was to abide by the rules.

We did have some down time in rehab, but it was nothing like county jail; it was always so loud. There was very little to no privacy. The bathrooms had no stall doors, only side ones. The showers were in one huge area that everyone had to share. The thought of using the bathroom mortified me. I never used to care about my body—I had never viewed it as a sacred vessel, and I had abused it when I was apart from Christ. But now it was different. God had washed me white as snow, and I wanted to protect my body and keep it holy, clean and pure. I think that's why the whole experience felt so humiliating.

I felt lost. The days here were much longer and harder, and I found it difficult to quiet my mind and focus on the Lord. I began to worry I had lost my salvation or that I was going to lose my faith. Since becoming a Christian, I hadn't gone for any extended period without a devoted 'quiet time' time with the Lord each day. Here, it was nearly impossible to drown out the constant noise so I could journal and read my Bible, and I had to capture brief moments to pray. Even when we walked, we had to march with our hands behind our back, chanting as we went.

In this facility, I was also further away from everyone back home. For the first thirty days no letters or visitors were allowed, but even beyond that I knew I wouldn't have many visitors due to the much longer distance from home and limited visitation hours. Though it was lonely, I was grateful to not have many visitors as the process felt so violating—every time we left for and returned from visitation, we were required to form a circle and undress to ensure no contraband was being smuggled in or out.

During our group sessions we sat in a large circle and shared about the circumstances that had brought us to the facility. I learned a lot during those sessions. I discovered that, in severe cases, addictive substances can stop the brain from growing and developing as it should. I also learned that once an addictive behavior starts, it's hard to quit because of the release of a chemical called dopamine in your brain. Dopamine affirms that a behavior feels good, but in time, this feeling of satisfaction becomes a need, until it becomes almost impossible to say no.

We also learned steps to help overcome addiction. Many women in rehab were mothers, and they missed their children greatly. They wanted to be good moms, but knew they had to change or they wouldn't have their babies in their lives for much longer. One of the very first steps was to change our environment. If someone wanted to break a drug addiction, they could not remain connected to the people they bought drugs from—they needed to get away and start over. But it had to come from the person themselves—if someone was not truly willing and desiring change, they could move away and still find themselves giving in to the same bad influences because they were unconsciously looking for them.

One of the most impactful things I learned, however, was that recovery centers or rehabilitation facilities typically only take addicts without insurance coverage for up to thirty days. Of course, thirty days is nowhere near enough time for someone to break free from a life of addiction—it is an ongoing process. And if those recovery centers are not Christ-centered, and people do not receive the hope that can only be found in Him, those who need help might struggle forever to break free from the chains of their addiction.

My heart broke as I thought about all the lives that had been impacted by addiction. Many of the people in my life were struggling with addiction—and still are to this day. I was very humbled to realise I was there, in the rehab facility, where I could get help. I hated it, and I often felt humiliated, but it stirred my heart knowing that God chose to save me, help me, and lead me away from destruction.

In the rehab facility we spent time discussing what we had done, and why we did it. In one session, we had to go back to the beginning and write down what was happening in our lives before things went wrong, then what happened in the lead-up to being arrested. Not everyone took these discussions seriously, however. Although I met some really great women in that place, I also met some not-so-great women. Some considered it all a joke, despite it being a punishment. One woman tried to fake a pregnancy during the intake by using a pregnant woman's pee sample. I couldn't believe it, but that's how it often is—some just do not get it, and some face more limitations than others before finally realizing there is a better way to live.

I knew I had broken the law and deserved to be there, but God had touched my life in a way that changed me. I was grateful God led me to His arms when He did—who knows where I might have ended up without Him? My mind no longer thought the way it did before; God had broken that destructive cycle through His love and presence. Now He was giving me the tools I needed to stay sober, and thankfully, although it was uncomfortable at times, I persevered because I valued the life Christ had in mind for me so much more.

I looked for Christ on campus everywhere, even though, for the first time in a long while, I couldn't 'feel' Him. When I looked outside and saw the heavens declaring His glory and His workmanship, I reminded myself He was still close. One evening, I was feeling depressed and far from God until I looked out of the window. It was like a beautiful painted picture. The trees were still, the sky was bursting with colors from orange to pink, and I felt such peace. In that moment, I thanked God for the beauty of His creation.

I remember a woman asking me soon after why I seemed so different. She was one of the troublemakers, and I often felt a bit intimidated by her strong personality. "Are you a nun or something?" she asked. "No, God has made me new," I told her. "He has taken my shame from me and given me a chance to start over." Even though I was feeling down, I knew this was a moment God had ordained. I may never know the full impact of that brief conversation, but it was evident that God was using me to plant spiritual seeds in these women's lives by sharing my testimony whenever I could. Even during the hard days, God was giving me opportunities to share His love, and I was grateful to take them.

I developed a high level of trust with the women in the rehab center—they knew I was different, and some of them shared more with me during our time there than they had ever shared with anyone else. Sharing our stories in a group setting was always very emotional, but it provided the greatest opportunity to connect with others on a deeper level. The youngest girl I connected with was eighteen years old, and she had a baby at home. I'd sing songs to her as we walked together, and she would feel such joy. Once, I was humming to myself, when a group of women asked if I would sing for them. I took advantage of the opportunity and sang the first thing that came to mind—"I love you, Lord." I wasn't trying to impress anyone but the Lord, but after I was finished, I opened my eyes and saw one woman with tears streaming down her face.

My hope was that each woman I encountered would come to know and experience the hope that I had found in Him. They looked to me for courage and for joy, though it wasn't me that could give it to them. I simply showed them what only Jesus could offer them.

These experiences might sound glorious—and some moments were, because God was in the midst of them—but I still struggled greatly. I had panic attacks, and at times I found it hard to trust

God. As Christmas approached, I began to feel particularly overwhelmed. I was crying one day as I was on my way to a check-in meeting with one of the advisors, because life felt so difficult for me. One of the faculty members stopped me and asked, "Don't you proclaim that you have faith in God?" I told him, "Yes, I do." He replied, "Then why do you have so little faith? Trust Him! If you are walking around gloomy with your head down and you have all these people watching you, do you think they are going to believe what you believe?" It was hard to hear, but he was right. I had to be strong.

Thankfully, God had ways of strengthening me even in my weakness. When I entered the advisor's office, I recognized the music that was playing on his computer. It was worship music, and right away, I knew it was a sign from God. It had been such a long time since I had been able to listen to any worship music that I just sat in the chair for a while and took it all in. Hearing that music was so refreshing to my soul. It was as though the Lord was giving me just what I needed to quench my thirst before heading back to the dorm.

That night, I reached out to Hurley, my friend from the warehouse, to ask if he would pray about something that had been troubling me. I had begun to feel the communication between my dad and I was breaking down—I couldn't put my finger on it, but the tone in his letters seemed to have changed since I had been transferred to the rehab facility. It was as if he was angry, and I had no idea why, but I was hesitant to call him. That night when Hurley answered the phone, it was almost as if he was expecting me to call. He prayed powerfully for me, asking God to give me peace and a sound mind, and the strength and comfort I needed to make it to the end. Hurley's letters had been a great encouragement to me—I would read them over and over while I was in there. It was such comfort to know that he was on my side and praying for me, especially when my relationship with my dad seemed to be deteriorating. When I reached out to him, I was beyond tired, but that prayer gave me the strength to endure. It was one of many small yet significant moments when the Lord spoke to me—moments when, if I hadn't been alert or waiting expectantly for His presence, I may have missed them.

My last days in the facility were nothing short of a miracle. When I graduated from the program and heard that I was finally going home, it felt like the greatest victory! Everyone who finished the program was given a special ceremony where they could choose someone to speak on their behalf as a sort of send-off into the real world. I had become very close to a woman who worked in the chapel on campus, and I chatted to her every time I saw her. She had a heart to serve the Lord, and I asked her to speak at my ceremony. She told the rest of the campus about how my faith in Christ had changed her drastically, and that once she left, she would continue to seek a relationship with Him. She wanted to have what I had!

Another woman spoke at my graduation ceremony as well—she had a good sense of humor, and we shared many laughs together. Even though I hadn't talked with her much about Jesus, she was drawn to me and often watched me to see how I would act around the others. She told everyone that mine was no 'jailhouse conversion', but that I was 'the real deal'. She said she knew that I truly loved God with all my heart and soul, that there were times when she was so angry she wanted to flip over a table or punch someone in the face, but then she would see my smile and know it was the wrong thing to do. With tears streaming down her face, she, too, said she wanted what I had. It was one of the most profound moments of my life. My time as an inmate was coming to an end, and it felt as though I had passed the test. My faith had kept me strong until the end.

Two days before Christmas, my dad and a close friend came to pick me up. Little did I know there was a group of people waiting for me at our friend's house to celebrate my homecoming. Truthfully, I was a bit embarrassed to see everyone. Typically, in a church environment, getting out of jail is not something you would think was worthy of celebration. Nevertheless, I arrived to a house filled with love and laughter and received a beautiful greeting. There were decorations everywhere, and even a cake to welcome me back. I couldn't believe I had such great people in my life. My pastor had a gift for me; it was a bracelet and a journal in which she'd written Jeremiah 29:11—one of the first verses I ever memorized as a Christian. I knew the Lord was confirming He had been with me through this recent chapter of my life. And He would continue to be with me through whatever came next, arming me with His strength.

The time I spent in rehabilitation was very difficult, yet reading the Bible was a fundamental practice in helping me overcome. When we stop searching or seeking in the midst of our pain, we lose all hope because we are disconnecting ourselves from our lifeline. When I was in jail, I read my Bible daily. I was a new Christian and even though I knew I was genuinely changed, I was surrounded by other criminals for four months! There are a lot of things that go on in these places, and it would have been easy for me to join in with the crowd and gravitate toward negative cycles of behavior. Still, I didn't do that. I kept my faith and trusted that God didn't send me there so I could lose my love for Him. Filling my spirit with God's Word was my anchor in the storm. I have pages and pages of verses that sustained me, and God used me in an amazing way while I was serving my time. He knew I would be obedient to Him, even in the fire.

During the months I spent in confinement, I would look at this Scripture that was taped next to my bed and tell myself, *He's making gold out of me, He's making gold out of me.* I walked out of the rehabilitation center on a spiritual high. I couldn't wait to see what the future held.

CHAPTER SEVEN

LIFE ON THE OUTSIDE

Before our release, my fellow inmates and I had spent a good portion of time talking about what we were going to do when we got out. We dreamed about the 'firsts'—the first thing we would eat or the first place we were going to go. All I knew, however, was that I wanted to go home.

Finally, I had made it! I had served my time; now I was excited to embark on the journey ahead. I was sure that things would feel better, be better—be different—than before. I was ready and determined to start fixing everything that was messed up, crooked, and backward in my life.

My expectations couldn't have been further from reality.

When I was released, it was like being propelled into a spiritually dry, desert place. I had presumed that once I was home, life would start looking up. I would finally meet the husband I had been praying for—and I would start serving again at my church. My church family had been such a wonderful support to me while I was in jail and had written many letters and postcards to encourage me. Now, I was just ready to get back to them all! I had especially missed the presence of God I always felt in the church, and I was excited to worship Him again without any reservations.

For a while, things went well. While I had been away, revival had broken out at my church. This was life-changing for a lot of those who had attended, and I was sad to have missed out even though I knew God was using me in a unique and amazing way on a mission for Him! Now that I had been released, I was excited to hear more about it and hopefully even experience it for myself.

I had grown up in a Pentecostal church, so when I was finally able to attend the revival services, I wasn't scared or intimidated by God's presence—I wanted to receive whatever He saw fit to give me! I wasn't disappointed. For the first time in my life, during those revival services, I felt complete freedom! In fact, I was so full of the presence of God that I lay on the floor and couldn't move! The revivalist, who was about the same age as me, laid his hands on my back. In that moment, God broke the stronghold of oppression that had been in my life since I was a child, and I was filled with an indescribable joy and received many promises from the Lord. It felt as though the weight of the world had been lifted from my shoulders. The heaviness of all my trials and burdens was gone. Finally, I was free!

We may not always understand the exact dynamics that hold us back from experiencing more freedom in Christ. The issue could stem from our flesh desiring control over our spirit, or from generational curses or even demonic influence. Thankfully, there is no need for despair. God is able to fully release us, restore us and equip us for ministry. Did you know that there is a woman in the Bible named Mary, who was plagued by demons? Jesus freed her, and she became one of His most devoted followers. In fact, she was the one who announced to the other disciples that Jesus had risen from the grave. In Luke's gospel we read:

> "Afterward he was traveling from one town and village to another, preaching and telling the good news of the kingdom of God. The Twelve were with him, and also some women who had been healed of evil spirits and sicknesses: Mary, called Magdalene (seven demons had come out of her); Joanna the wife of Chuza, Herod's steward; Susanna; and many others who were supporting them from their possessions."
>
> **Luke 8:1-3**

Talk about deliverance! It's important to note that although the word 'deliverance' might make us think of a dramatic experience, with shaking or convulsions or people throwing themselves to the ground, this is not always the case. Deliverance can also come gradually as we continue to walk with Jesus. It is not limited to those who are plagued with 'seven devils' or don't know Jesus—deliverance is for us all.

The apostle Paul wrote about this in his letter to the Romans:

> "Therefore do not let sin reign in your mortal body, so that you obey its desires. And do not offer any parts of it to sin as weapons for unrighteousness. But as those who are alive from the dead, offer yourselves to God, and all the parts of

yourselves to God as weapons for righteousness. For sin will not rule over you, because you are not under the law but under grace."

Romans 6:12-14

For me, this was the hard part—learning how to live free and remain free. The healing and deliverance I had experienced at the revival was lifechanging—especially as it coincided with the end of my sentence. But the revival didn't last. Now I needed to learn to walk in my newfound freedom.

There comes a time when we must learn how to truly live out our faith and walk in the freedom we have been given. The reality of this can be mundane—and flat-out exhausting—especially when there are still consequences to be faced! But God always has a greater purpose for us. His presence is a force of nature that pierces through the hidden details and agendas of our hearts to propel us into greater things.

After the revival ended, I found a new and profound strength and developed a deeper understanding of who Christ is. I also realized that God takes us through a process of preparing us for the 'greater things' that are to come. And these greater things are worth waiting for.

I had a lot of things to work through, however, before God would propel me forward into the greater purposes He had planned for me. As the novelty of all the 'firsts' wore off, I realized I still had to face the reality of my consequences. I had to pay attention to everything I was doing to make sure I stayed out of trouble and kept my life on track. The next few months and even years would be quite a challenge. I was out of the rehabilitation center, but I was still on probation, and it was vitally important I abide by the conditions I had been given. I didn't want to drink, or be around anyone who drank, and I certainly didn't want to be in a place where there might be any type of drugs. Suffice to say, the challenges I endured in jail and the state rehab facility were small in comparison to the changes that I was about to face.

For a start, my relationship with God felt different after I was released from jail. It seemed He wasn't as close to me as He had been before. As a result, I often felt drained and exhausted, and there were many days I just wanted to give up. Yet God didn't give up on me. He sees the big picture, even when we cannot. And He was incredibly faithful with the details of my everyday circumstances.

I was fortunate that when I returned to work in the warehouse it was as though I had never left. Before going to jail, I had to let my boss know where I would be for four months. They knew about my situation, but they also knew I loved God and was committed to my church. Then, unexpectedly, just one week before I left to serve my sentence, we got a new supervisor in our department—a man I believe God placed there at just the right time to benefit me. Until that point, I had not been a model employee. I worked hard when I was there. I was open to learning different areas, and to training people. However, more often than not, I felt like I was a mess at work. I was often late, I had a lot of family issues, and I struggled with anxiety. If I'm being honest, I didn't know what hard work truly was until I became a Christian. Even so, my new supervisor did not hesitate for a moment when I told him I was about to go to jail. "You will have your job when you get out," he assured me. What a blessing! I belonged to Christ, and because of that, I believe I received supernatural favor!

When I had finished serving my time and returned to work, Hurley was still there. Hurley was no saint (as he told me when he shared his stories), but he genuinely cared for me and was a bright light in a dark time. He was the one I had called when I was most desperate in the rehab facility, and he was there for me as I adjusted to my new life afterwards. Hurley's grandson had a car sitting in his yard for years but was unable to drive. When I got out of the rehab center, Hurley asked his grandson for the car, and he gave it to him. Hurley then fixed it all up at a cost of eight or nine hundred dollars, then told me he was going to give *me* the car! I couldn't believe it! I had prayed fervently to God for a vehicle before going to jail, but I had no idea how it could ever happen. Imagine my disbelief when I found he had a car waiting for me, tagged and registered, complete with a full tank of gas, the first month's insurance paid in full, and new windscreen wipers! It was simply a testament to the goodness of God!

Do you know what else happened? One day, I visited the local Christian bookstore looking for a Bible. I wanted to find a special one but couldn't decide which one to get. An older couple noticed I was looking at bibles and felt led to go away and pray for a minute. When they returned, they bought a Bible for me and even arranged to have my name engraved on it! They said that when they prayed, God told them to buy the Bible for me!

So many good things were happening in my life! I started helping with a homeless ministry and was able to share my testimony of what God had done for me. One day, as I was praying for a woman, she took drugs and a crack pipe out of her pocket and immediately threw them away!

The goodness of God was so tangible during this time. Since saying yes to Jesus and trusting Him with every detail of my life, I received unbelievable blessings—things I never could have imagined. In every circumstance He has gone before me and made a way—even when it seemed hopeless. His providence never ceases to amaze me. I love what Psalm 84 says about God's favor towards His people:

> "Oh God . . . show favor to the one you have anointed. A single day in your courts is better than a thousand anywhere else! I would rather be a gatekeeper in the house of my God, than live the good life in the homes of the wicked. For the Lord God is our sun and our shield. He gives us grace and glory. The Lord will withhold no good thing from those who do what is right. O LORD of Heaven's Armies, what joy for those who trust in you."
>
> **Psalm 84:9-12, NLT**

Everything about my time in jail had been hard, but my 'mission trip to Arkansas' had forever changed me. Before I went away, I remember praying, *Show me your heart, Lord. I want to be used the way you used the disciples. I want to be able to heal people in your name and show them without a doubt that God is real.* I am here to tell you that God answered my prayer and used me in that place to touch women's hearts. It was nothing short of a miracle, but this was God's plan for me all along. He took my punishment and used it in ways I could never have imagined.

One of those ways was how God used my time in jail to awaken the hearts of my church family. I felt like a modern-day Paul sending letters to my church about the things I was experiencing. I shared with them how my heart broke for the women in the facility and the hardships they had endured, and how I was sure God had sent me there to listen to their stories and to shine the light of Jesus. My dad read the letters aloud to my pastors, and when they shared my news with the church, there wasn't a dry eye in the house. How humbling it was to think that my experience in jail had encouraged *others* in their faith!

Still, despite the blessings, adjusting to my newfound freedom was not an easy transition. It could have been because of my depression or anxiety, or even that my perspective had changed a lot since coming home—I don't truly know. But I do know the enemy was nearby, desperate to wreak havoc in my life and distract me from the Lord in whatever way he could.

One of these areas was in my relationship with my dad. He had expectations for me once I got out that I wasn't ready for, and because of this, he was angry with me. Eventually I moved out of his house and moved in with a couple from my church, but even then, we continued to have ridiculous fights over the phone that left me feeling stressed and in despair. My dad even left the church that we had been going to together on a weekly basis. I couldn't believe that despite all the amazing ways God was blessing my life, my relationship with my dad was taking a turn for the worse. God would need to do a mighty work to reconcile our fractured relationship, and it would take a lot of time to repair the damage that had been done. In the meantime, however, every day was a struggle.

My financial situation was particularly stressful. Although my dad had been able to arrange some insurance, I still had to pay outstanding bills for the claims filed against me before I went to jail. Mercifully, I didn't have to pay rent, but paying two hundred and fifty dollars a month toward those bills on top of the debt I was trying to manage was incredibly overwhelming. I wasn't able to even open my own checking account because of my previous irresponsible behavior, and my credit report was extremely damaging. It all left me feeling unbelievably anxious, and for a long time I couldn't see past the mountain of mistakes I had created for myself.

Work was also very difficult, and after a while I didn't want to be at my job anymore. A lot of the guys I worked with would come up to me and make inappropriate comments. I could laugh and brush off most of them, but one comment was so disgusting I decided to report it. That was when things *really* took a turn for the worse. I was transferred from one department to another and moved all over the place, but I couldn't see the point. It didn't appear to be making any difference. I went back and forth with God, questioning whether I needed to stay at work. "Lord, help me!" I prayed. I needed His wisdom and discernment, and I needed the paycheck—I couldn't risk missing a debt payment and ending up back in Arkansas, or even worse, jail.

This was such a trying time for me that I even had to fight to go to church. There were times I would try to talk myself out of it. *I'm too tired. I've been working sixty hours a week. They don't need me there on Wednesday nights anyway.* Thankfully, the couple I was living with at the time encouraged me to make the effort, but it was still an uphill battle.

I began to have more and more bad days. I hated that my dad and I weren't talking and that our relationship wasn't working out, and I felt so depressed thinking *this* was the life I would always have.

It came to a head one day—I was ready to quit work, but just as I was about to hand in my notice, a dear friend from church encouraged me. He told me he had been having a hard time himself, but that he too needed to stay at his job until he could find something else. He gave me this analogy:

There once was a man who was told by his supervisor to move a rock. Every day, he would get up, roll up his sleeves, and start pushing. Finally, he went to the supervisor and said, "I'm done! I cannot do this anymore! The rock is not moving! It won't even budge. Why would you have me do this?" Then the supervisor said, "Look at your arms. They are stronger! Look at your legs. You've been trying to push this rock daily—look how strong your legs have gotten!" The man realized all his effort was not for nothing. Each day as he pressed forward, he gained strength that he didn't know he had.

That story was the wake-up call I needed. I hadn't realized it, but through it all God was strengthening my character. He was using my trials and difficult circumstances to prepare me for what lay ahead. He had plans and purposes for my future that I could never imagine! I just had to keep walking in faith and trust that He would be faithful to keep His promises in my life.

CHAPTER EIGHT

THE ROAD TO WHOLENESS

The first few years after leaving the rehabilitation center were difficult, but gradually I learned how to manage my responsibilities, develop a steady relationship with the Lord, and maintain consistent accountability in my life (not just when *I* wanted it). I was growing, maturing, and increasing in my ability to handle the bigger things God had called me to.

One of the keys to this growth was finding healing from my past. For many years I had been unable to move forward—it was as if I was stuck in my old ways and sin patterns. One of the reasons for this was my tendency to keep my problems to myself. I had never sought help from others. I had carried so many concerns, but I wouldn't talk to professionals who could help me, and even pushed away my closest friends. As a result, I had not received the healing I so desperately needed as I grew up. I had been so used to doing things on my own, but as I found the courage to trust others to speak into my life, I began to see that ever since my parents had divorced when I was a little girl, I'd carried a lot on my shoulders.

For anyone who has gone through any form of trauma, I hugely recommend meeting with a counselor who is aligned with the Word of God or someone in your church who is a part of a healing ministry and asking them to pray with you. It is a life-changing process.

It was my pastors who walked alongside me as I adjusted to life on the other side of jail. They became true friends to me, gently but intentionally speaking into my life, encouraging me, and helping me stay in alignment with God's purposes for me. They were my mentors. They also prayed over me.

One time when I was on the worship team at church, my pastor came over to me while we were worshipping. He laid his hands on my shoulders and quietly said, "Let it go." It was a pivotal moment in my healing journey.

My pastors also helped me understand how to manage my finances. With debts to pay off and such a limited income, tithing felt impossible, but my pastors reminded me of the spiritual principle of tithing. I needed a breakthrough in my finances though, and so from my very next paycheck, I began giving ten percent to the Lord. I am convinced that bringing our 'ten percent into the storehouse' (Malachi 3:10) unlocks heaven's blessings in every area of our lives. From the day I first started giving to the Lord until now, I have never been without a job, a vehicle, or a place to live.

One of the most challenging areas for me, however, was my desire for a husband. When I first became a Christian, I had two big prayer requests. The first was that God would help me find a husband. The second was that I would be able to pay off my debts. At the time, both seemed impossible, far-off dreams. Sure enough, God didn't give me what I asked right away. Perhaps He knew I needed time to prepare myself practically and spiritually for these future blessings.

Meanwhile, the most important priority for me was maintaining a strong relationship with Jesus. Then, I had to focus on doing what was right, working to pay off my debts, and managing my responsibilities. As young adults who want to do big things for the Lord, these tasks can seem mundane, even pointless. We don't want to deal with them because they aren't fun! Having a boyfriend or girlfriend is fun. Hanging out with friends is fun. There is nothing wrong with any of those things. Yet our consistent obedience in the small things attracts the attention of Jesus. The Word of God tells us that if God can trust us with little, He can trust us with a lot (Luke 16:10-12). Therefore, if we as believers want to be authentic—I mean, the 'real deal'—we also need to be faithful in our daily steps of practical obedience.

I knew this, but still I let my guard down in the area I struggled with most—relationships. When I started going back to church, I connected with a man who was recently divorced and had a daughter, and he soon started pursuing a relationship with me. I honestly wasn't sure if I was ready for all of that. On our first date, I even cried, because any form of touch was uncomfortable for me. All he did was kiss me on the cheek, but when I got home, it felt like my heart had been ripped open.

Pursuing that relationship was not the right decision. Throughout my life I have failed many times, and this was one of those times. I should have had clear boundaries, and I didn't. Instead, I got sucked into the patterns of the 'old Syprina'—the one who was a slave to lust. Within this relationship, all I could focus on were the words of Paul in 1 Corinthians:

> "... if they can't control themselves they should go ahead and marry. It's better to marry than to burn with lust."
>
> **1 Corinthians 7:9, NLT**

Obviously, marrying wasn't the answer—healing was—yet I kept getting sucked into this strong conviction that it would be better for us to be married. I couldn't get rid of it, and I felt trapped. I was still working to pay off my debt and since he was paying me to watch his daughter on the weekends, I convinced myself this relationship was helping me toward my goals.

I should have allowed more time for God to do the heart work in me before getting involved with a man. But I didn't. I felt terrible for this man and his daughter's situation, and I wanted to help. I understood what my boyfriend's daughter was going through because my parents also got divorced when I was little, and I wanted to show her the love of Jesus. In so doing, however, I failed to take responsibility for what *I* needed to do in my own situation. I was paying my debt, but I was failing miserably at paying rent. I didn't have a stable home (after moving out of my dad's house, I stayed with three different people), and I eventually left the warehouse job because I felt God was leading me elsewhere. I ended up working in three other places after I left, and it was all just a mess. Rather than seeking help, I suffered in silence with my financial issues and even made things worse when I got a title loan on the car Hurley had purchased for me. Hurley was disappointed. He told me I better not ever do that again, then he helped me to pay it off.

Things eventually got to the point where I needed to find another place to live, but I didn't know what to do. I didn't have money saved up, nor did I know anyone else I could move in with. At the same time, my boyfriend was looking for a house. He told me we were going to get married eventually, and he was tired of seeing me living with everyone else and it not working out, so he asked me to move in with him.

Even though I had made mistakes in this relationship, God's conviction in me was strong. I knew it wasn't the right thing to do, and I didn't want to move in with him. The Holy Spirit was guiding me, and I was grateful for that. Even so, I decided to act against my better judgment, and it felt like there were no other options, so I moved in with him and his daughter. I told my boyfriend I wasn't keen on the arrangement and that it would be a temporary situation until I found another place to live. I ensured we would sleep in separate rooms, but that didn't make it easier! In fact, it was hell on earth. Our spirits collided. He didn't understand what it meant to 'wait before marriage', and this was a struggle for him. Living with someone you are not married to when you are a Christian desiring to do the right thing would be a struggle for anyone—that's why you're not supposed to cohabit until you are married. For us, it became a daily battle, physically and spiritually. It wasn't working, and I wasn't surprised because I knew it was wrong. Finally, I found another place to stay. When I packed up everything to leave, I was more than ready to go.

My plan was to go into a transitional housing program for ninety days. To qualify, I had to be working full-time, and there were strict rules which were enforced to stop residents from spending more than they should. You couldn't get your nails done or highlights in your hair, and they limited all other expenses. Getting into the program was hard—I had to call every day, asking for my name to be moved up the list, until finally I was accepted. Yet when I was eventually offered a place, fear held me back. I didn't believe that I could succeed in this new environment, and I *really* didn't want to fail. I had my car packed up and I was ready to meet someone about the apartment, but I was afraid, and my fear won in the end.

All along, my boyfriend was telling me that he didn't want me to go. I reminded him that he had said we would get married, and it wasn't happening. He promised that if I stayed, we would get married, and we would look at rings within a week. In the moment, I believed him, and I stayed. I knew I was supposed to go; I *should have* gone. But I didn't, and I missed my opportunity.

Friends, we got married within three months. It wasn't delightful. We weren't ready. I had finally managed to pay off all my other debts, but I still carried the financial burden of paying probation fees each month and paying off the restitution from Arkansas. But God was faithful, even though I wasn't being faithful to Him. He cared for me and was still working through all the trials I was facing.

I still didn't truly understand the kind of love God had for me, and because of that, I got married before I was ready to. Since then, my husband and I have had to overcome many obstacles, and sometimes I wish I could go back in time and fix it. That's why it's so important to obey the promptings God places in our hearts and to be convinced of what God says about who we are and why He has made us. It's an essential part of our deliverance—finding our true identity in Him.

Thankfully, God has the final say and He works everything for good—even if we mess up. He will *always* choose us! But if we are to keep moving forward, we must cling by faith to the Word of God.

I was blessed that, while I was in jail, the Word of God became a lifeline to my soul. As I read and studied the scriptures, I came to know Jesus in a deeper way and found strength to hold on even when the days became unimaginably hard. Before I went to jail, God had given me a verse, which He directly fulfilled in my life:

> "My word that comes from my mouth will not return to me empty, but it will accomplish what I please and will prosper in what I send it to do."
>
> **Isaiah 55:11**

God was fulfilling His Word to me, but I also needed to be obedient to His Word. Psalm 119:9-11 says,

> "How can a young man keep his way pure? By keeping your word. I have sought you with all my heart; don't let me wander from your commands. I have treasured your word in my heart so that I may not sin against you."

I needed to treasure God's Word just like the psalmist. God wanted to keep me from sin, but also from separation from Himself, feeling far away from Him. In the Bible we read:

> "But your iniquities are separating you from your God, and your sins have hidden his face from you so that he does not listen."
>
> **Isaiah 59:2**

Sin is the only thing that keeps us distant from God, but faith in Him and His Word will keep us close to Him. Whatever difficulty or trial you face, this can be your experience too. What has God asked you to do? Trust that God is right there with you and will use every situation for your good. Even though it may not seem so at times, He has so much in store for you and He is always with you, watching over you—even in the harshest of places. In the words of Deuteronomy 32:10:

> "He found them in a desert land, in an empty, howling wasteland. He surrounded them and watched over them; he guarded them as he would guard his own eyes" (NLT).

The Lord watches over His people! When we focus our attention on earthly things instead of God's Word, it causes us to stumble.

I cannot tell you how many times I wanted to leave my boyfriend before I got married, but my fear held me back. Even though I knew the relationship was becoming an obstacle to my faith, I stayed. It was the same with my relationship with my dad—I let our conversations affect my behavior because I was not confident in what God's Word said about me. The truth is my low self-esteem was keeping me from believing what God said about me and what He wanted to do for me.

Every time I put my trust in anything or anyone other than God, my self-worth took a nosedive. My negative thoughts would eat away at me—and they skewed my perception of God, too. Still, they swirled in my mind, as if on repeat:

> *Whoa, God, I didn't know I had so much anger in me.*
> *I had no idea I was so insecure.*
> *God, I hate myself.*
> *I didn't realize I was letting them take advantage of me. I'm so weak.*
> *I'm so worthless, I must deserve this.*
> *If they think I'm worthless, you must think I'm worthless.*

Of course, my feelings of worthlessness could not have been further from the truth. God doesn't want us to be bound by what other people say about us—He wants us to belong to Him, convinced of who we are as children of the King. When we face a trial with our eyes fixed on God, our perspective changes, and our questions lead us deeper into His heart for us:

How does He see me in this storm?

What does God want to do in me during this trial?

What is His purpose for me while I'm walking in this chaos?

How is God using this time to prepare me for the future blessings He has for me?

I am not always the most rational thinker when I'm in the middle of the trial, and maybe you're not either. Usually, I haven't been able to fully understand what God was doing in me until long after the storm has passed. Yet something miraculous happens once we come out the other side. We get to start over!

For me, starting over felt like climbing Mount Everest for the first time. It was an uphill battle. Yet I will always be thankful for the opportunity God gave me to start again. Having faith gave me a new perspective and a new way of living. We cannot do the new things God offers us if we are not willing to let go of our old ways of living.

In the Old Testament, we read that Abraham had to leave all that was familiar to him in order to pursue the promises of God for his life. The same is true for us. And just like Abraham, God gives us grace to make the transitions. Abraham didn't know where he was going, but God granted him the grace to get there. When God was leading me, I had to leave my old life behind too. Everything that would keep me attached to the world I had known, needed to go. *Why?* Because God wanted and desired my identity to be found in Him alone.

Some people appear to follow Jesus, but they remain the same person they were before they were saved. There are also people who are willing to do whatever it takes to follow God's will for their lives. These people leave relationships that are not good for them. They leave family and friends behind for a greater purpose in Christ. They aren't ashamed. They aren't defeated. Instead, they continue to pursue the righteousness of God.

It's a big ask, yet God is just as concerned with our small steps of obedience as He is with the big ones. He will highlight the areas we need to work on as we seek His will. Personally, I have learned that being connected with an accountability partner while navigating the circumstances of my life is crucial. Only by remaining open to guidance and correction are we able to achieve the success we need to thrive in our future families and ministry.

I encourage you to seek God and follow His lead, no matter what He asks. He knows you and He loves you. He can accomplish great things through you if you simply trust Him.

CHAPTER NINE

SAYING GOODBYE TO FEAR

It is empowering to look back on our trials and see how God brought us safely through to the other side of the struggles. At times like that we feel we can conqueror anything. I imagine Paul felt this way at the end of his life. Look at what he says in *The Message* translation:

> "Because of the extravagance of those revelations, and so I wouldn't get a big head, I was given the gift of a handicap to keep me in constant touch with my limitations. Satan's angel did his best to get me down; what he in fact did was push me to my knees. No danger then of walking around high and mighty! At first I didn't think of it as a gift, and begged God to remove it. Three times I did that, and then he told me, *My grace is enough; it's all you need. My strength comes into its own in your weakness.*

Once I heard that, I was glad to let it happen. I quit focusing on the handicap and began appreciating the gift. It was a case of Christ's strength moving in on my weakness. Now I take limitations in stride, and with good cheer, these limitations that cut me down to size—abuse, accidents, opposition, bad breaks. I just let Christ take over! And so the weaker I get, the stronger I become."

2 Corinthians 12:7-10, MSG

There are two paths we can take when we face difficult seasons. The first is to trust that we will experience God's strength and goodness amid the trial. The second path is to look only to our own strength to endure. I know I have attempted both scenarios. Without a doubt, however, the burden feels substantially bigger when I believe I can persevere independently, apart from God. I become overwhelmed, and I only end up having to apologize to people I hurt along the way. Sometimes I still struggle with this. It's impossible to carry the weight of life on our own and still think that we are walking in Christ and modeling His love to others.

Carrying my own load wasn't something I ever tried to do intentionally. It has been a defense mechanism I developed over time that I thought I needed for survival. Trauma can cause us to think we *have to* do things on our own because our bodies have become accustomed to responding to difficulty in the way they always have. But when we are walking in righteousness, we no longer have to respond the way we did before. We can choose to be overwhelmed, convinced we must carry our burdens alone, or we can look to Jesus, who is "able to do above and beyond all that we ask or think according to the power that works in us" (Ephesians 3:20).

Jesus is more than able to carry every burden—every betrayal, every deception, every pain, and every heavy wound. With each blow that pierced His hands and His feet, all of it was nailed to the cross. Until Jesus breathed His last breath, He bore all these things on our behalf—not because He was *evil,* but because He was so *good.* He had to be the One to carry these things for us, because He was the only One who could defeat the demonic influences over our lives. And so, when Jesus died on the cross, all these things that harm us *died with Him.* He paid the ultimate price, so that we could ultimately be overcomers too.

Friend, when we lay all our trials, heartache, pain, anger and resentment at the feet of Jesus, we are telling the devil he has no power over us anymore. Instead, we are trusting that when Christ died on the cross, we gained the victory over all sin and darkness. Furthermore, these things were defeated so we could have a right relationship with God. As we read in 1 Timothy 2:5-6:

> "For there is one God and one mediator between God and mankind, the man Christ Jesus, who gave himself as a ransom for all, a testimony at the proper time."

The enemy may try to trick us and lie to us, telling us we are weak and worthless, that we have no hope and no God, but the truth is, it is the devil who has been ultimately defeated through the resurrection of Christ. We can break the stronghold he has over our life only through our faith in Christ. When we believe in Christ despite what we see (Hebrews 11:1), we defeat the enemy's plans and dismantle his authority over our lives. To do this takes true repentance.

Remember Abraham? As he left behind his old life and began walking in obedience to God, something incredible happened. God promised him that he would have as many descendants as there are stars in the sky (Genesis 26:4). That was a big deal! Abraham did eventually become the "father of many nations" and "the father of us all" (Romans 4:16, 17) but it didn't happen overnight. He and his wife Sarah had to wait for many years to see the promise fulfilled. Nevertheless, their faith remained strong. In Romans 4 we read:

> "Even when there was no reason for hope, Abraham kept hoping—believing that he would become the father of many nations. For God had said to him, "That's how many descendants you will have!" And Abraham's faith did not weaken, even though, at about 100 years of age, he figured his body was as good as dead—and so was Sarah's womb. Abraham never wavered in believing God's promise. In fact, his faith grew stronger, and in this he brought glory to God. He was fully convinced that God is able to do whatever he promises."
>
> **Romans 4:18-21, NLT**

Abraham walked through many difficulties, but these difficulties led him to a place in his life where God's promise of a son would come to fruition. In the process, Abraham's character was being built. As Abraham trusted God, God refined the imperfections and impurities within him, and when he had the proper heart posture, it was time. Sure enough, Abraham and Sarah had a son, and within a few generations, God worked out what seemed impossible for them to accomplish on their own. What an encouraging reminder that God is faithful through it all. He doesn't miss a moment as we go through His refining process!

If our goal is to finish the race well *and* for God to perfect our faith, we must be prepared to face situations that shape our character to become more and more like Christ. I can tell you that when I'm the middle of the process, it's often easy to forget what God has already done for me. "What are you doing?" I ask Him. "What did I do wrong?" Then I realize He is likely working some other things out in my soul or mind or heart. Friends, trials are how we continue to grow! Trials are how we become more like Him!

Perhaps you're wondering what to do when things get *really* difficult? I know some of you may have lost someone you loved deeply, battled addiction, faced infidelity in your marriage, or even been through divorce. Perhaps you feel like there is no hope in your situation. I do not ever wish to discredit the pain these situations bring, but I do want you to know that Jesus laid down His life so that you could have ultimate victory over every one of these trials. No matter what it is you have to walk through, if you keep your eyes and heart focused on God, you can trust He will be faithful and carry you through it all until His promises are fulfilled.

All through the Old Testament, the Bible gives us a clear example of what it looked like when people didn't put their trust in Him.

They eventually died. The lesson is clear: we can die spiritually when we don't cling to Christ during the difficulties of life.

Let's ask God in this very moment to forgive our unbelief. We can, right now, ask Him to forgive us for believing the enemy's lies instead of His truth. It doesn't matter how long it might take us to reach this point of repentance—He will be waiting. Believe me, it is so worth it. There is a greater purpose for all of us who choose to disarm the enemy's lies over our lives and lay down every burden at the feet of Jesus Christ!

∼

I have had many impossible obstacles in my life. I remind myself of where I used to be and how tragic my life would have been if I had never found Jesus. I remember how depressed I used to be in that there were times I even wanted to die, and I realize that God has delivered me over and over. He has not failed me. Ever.

When I struggle to understand why certain things are happening to me, or I am confused about the work God may be doing in my life or my character, I ask Him to reveal Himself and His purposes to me through His Word. He *always* shows me.

I've found evidence of God everywhere—when I worship, when I pray, and when I read the Bible. There were times I didn't want to read my Bible or go to church, but I still did it anyway because I didn't want to fall back into my old ways and give the devil a foothold in my life. I constantly had to remind myself of the testimony the Lord gave me—that I've never had a desire to drink again, I've never wanted to get myself into debt again where I couldn't get out of it, and I've managed to correct my faulty, destructive thinking. Even though I've messed up a lot along the way, it didn't throw me off track. By His grace I have remained connected to Christ, and in Him I have overcome . . . a lot! I love God now too much to ever go back to my old ways.

I still struggle at times with who God says I am compared to what others say about me. In the midst of trying situations I've had to silence the lies that tell me:

I'm not good enough.
I am what people say about me.
I will never overcome.
I will always be stuck.

Fear still tries to creep into my life sometimes. Yet I've learned that fear is ultimately a liar. Joyce Meyer describes fear using the acronym: False Evidence Appearing Real. This is so powerful! The things we think about ourselves that go against what God says about us are examples of false evidence appearing real. It's all a lie! The enemy wants to do whatever he can to keep us from God. He will convince us that God doesn't love us and that He's no longer around when we need Him the most.

Faith is so important to cling to when we are struggling. Where there is fear or uncertainty, remember your faith. Remember the testimony of what the Lord has done for you, and the faith that drew you in at the beginning. If you do not think you have that testimony or you aren't there yet, I encourage you to read Hebrews chapter eleven in the Bible. In this "faith chapter" you will be inspired by everyday heroes who didn't give up on their faith, despite incredible odds.

I encourage you to write out your testimony. When we take the time to write down and remember what Christ has done for us, it identifies us! It gives us written documentation that proves we no longer belong to the world, but to God. We are chosen! He made us holy through His Son! Christ gave us hope to hold onto so we can make it through every trial. God doesn't need to be reminded about what He has done for us, but He is magnified in our circumstances when we thank Him for saving us. Our faith comes alive by remembering.

Looking back in faith helps me see that every trial I've endured through Him has transformed me for the better. Now I worship Him from a heart that has been changed. By His grace, I have made it through the difficulties and now understand His love for me in a deeper way. Oh, how He loves me! He loves me dearly, and I know that more and more through every season. It can be hard to understand this love as we go through the process of deliverance, but 1 John 4:18 tells us that His perfect love casts out all fear. God *is* love, and we are safe in Him. His love can conquer *any* evil we face.

In Christ, we become more alive than ever, despite what we must go through along the way. He is our hope, He brings us healing, and He brings dead things back to life! Friends, He's holding and keeping us even when we cannot see it. He makes a way when there is no way! He opens doors that no man can close. He is the light that illuminates the path ahead. When we feel defeated,

He is our hope, even in the darkest valley. When the war rages within us, He is able to calm the storm.

Never in my life have I met anyone quite like Jesus. When something goes wrong, He has shown me His favor. When people are tearing me down, He blesses me with more of His presence. When I cannot take it anymore, He leads me to cast all my fears on Him. I know I can overcome every difficulty with Him. He's never left my side. The more I have pressed in to get to know Him, the more He has changed my life. And He can change your life, too.

Even at this very moment, He desires to be your light, your way, and your truth! He has the power to guide, heal, and mold your life for a greater purpose than you can ever imagine. And He is more than enough. Reflect on these words from Psalm 23:

> "Yahweh is my best friend and my shepherd. I always have more than enough. He offers a resting place for me in his luxurious love. His tracks take me to an oasis of peace near the quiet brook of bliss. That's where he restores and revives my life. He opens before me the right path and leads me along his footsteps of righteousness so that I can bring honor to his name. Even when your path takes me through the valley of deepest darkness, fear will never conquer me, for you already have! Your authority is my strength and my peace. The comfort of your love takes away my fear. I'll never be lonely, for you are near."
>
> **Psalm 23:1-4, TPT**

If you think He's not there with you, think again! He is the glue that can put all your broken pieces back together, and He can and will create a beautiful masterpiece with the broken pieces of your life. So, hold on, friend. God can and will make beauty out of ashes! Beginning again is possible, and He has wonderful things in store for those who trust in Him. Please don't quit.

CHAPTER TEN

A TRANSFORMED LIFE

When I began my walk with the Lord, I never imagined God would use my testimony in such a powerful way. For me, it has never been about boasting or wanting to put my story out there for my own glory. As I walked this journey of faith, I discovered just how big my God is, and my heart is to simply share what I know to be true about Him. He is a God who dances with me when I need to feel loved. He is a God who sings songs of deliverance over me when I can't fight anymore.

God has, without a doubt, saved me, changed me from the inside out, and showed me exactly what a new beginning looks like. I have started over, and over . . . and over again, and though this whole process looked nothing like I thought it would, by God's grace I can stand here today and testify to the unequivocal goodness of God in my life.

He has been kind to me in every circumstance. Knowing God has been the best thing that has happened to me. Not one person has been able to persuade me to give up on God or to go back to my old lifestyle. He has held me when I couldn't walk by myself, and no matter how far from Him I have felt at times, He's always been a constant presence. Psalm 139 says,

> "Where can I go to escape your Spirit? Where can I flee from your presence? If I go up to heaven, you are there; if I make my bed in Sheol, you are there. If I fly on the wings of the dawn and settle down on the western horizon, even there your hand will lead me; your right hand will hold on to me."
> **Psalm 139:7-10**

Once I found this presence, I never wanted to lose it. His presence changes everything; it is a constant rhythm of discovery. I pray that you would seek God's presence, too, because if you seek Him with all your heart, you will find Him (Jeremiah 29:13) and experience His tangible presence for yourself. It will give you the strength you need to make it through.

For me, the road is still not an easy one. I have faced many challenges, even after my new beginning. Yet through it all, God has held me. He has stayed so close. There were days when I wondered if I could ever get past the darkness, but I turned to God's Word to sustain me. I would cry out to Him, "God, I just can't take it anymore! I need you to speak to me or I won't make it!"

Over and over again, God answered me. He would speak to me at just the right time with just the right word. He has never failed me. There have been times that have been so difficult that

I needed to fast, pray for deliverance, and have a team praying with me. When I did everything that I possibly could, and had nothing left to give, God simply asked me to be still and trust Him. After everything that I've been through, I didn't think I could ever trust anyone fully again.

Throughout this whole journey, God has never left me or forsaken me. It has been a decade of overcoming heart issues and allowing my life to align with the truth of the written Word of God. In my relationship with my dad, I had to trust God to break down walls. We both have had to forgive many times. We've stayed silent, we've prayed and tried again. Our relationship isn't perfect, but we are at a perfect place to have a healthy relationship and communicate what we may be going through without judgment, and we have a force who stands with us when we come together to pray for our family. This is trusting Christ with everything, and not throwing in the towel too soon. It's a relationship restored and it's a testimony I can and will forever glean from in my other relationships that still need restoration.

I can tell you today with great joy that I am finally free! I'm free from all my debt—financially and spiritually—that came from my past. I no longer hold that burden over my head of wondering if it will ever end. I have endured ten years of probation and never once got into trouble again. I often wondered, *Why on earth, God, did I have to wait ten years to be completely free?* Well, God knew what He was doing. The week I lost my stepdad, I paid the final balance I owed for my restitution. The family I thought I could never experience reconciliation with, was able to share with me in this victory. God is so good! Now, I know God has everything fully under His control. He works everything out in His perfect timing, and He is never late. Every supposed 'delay' is another opportunity He gives us to wait for Him in faith.

I know if you are standing in difficulty right now, it may be hard to see the picture clearly. Just because I have overcome this trial, and God has fully restored the family relationships I thought I had lost during my criminal past, there are still things the Lord is working on within *me*. If you know that He is working on things in you too, I want you to be encouraged that you can make it through! Just trust and believe Him in the circumstances you are facing right now.

I was on a destructive path before I had an authentic relationship with Jesus, but even with Jesus some destructive behavior needed to be changed. I have made some awful, ungodly choices, some I would never mention to anyone before I knew Christ. Maybe you have been through something like this. Is there some darkness you have gone through that has left you with feelings of worthlessness? Do you feel lost like I was? Do you wonder if it's possible for you to begin again? God declares:

> "For I know the plans I have for you . . . plans for your well-being, not for disaster, to give you a future and a hope."
>
> **Jeremiah 29:11**

God is in the business of bringing dead things back to life (Romans 4:17). He is the God of new beginnings. When you let go of the fears that you are currently facing, know this: God is committed to you. He's committed to your process. Though you might want to give up, He will not. He stands strong for us and is always in our corner. He fights our battles for us.

There are many people right now who feel alone, afraid, and not sure how to start over. I want you to know that God knows everything about you. He sees the marriage you are in, the debt you carry, the brokenness, the addictions, the anger, and the shame. He's not mad at you; He loves you, and He wants you to go to Him. If you are experiencing pain and you don't know who to turn to, the best place you can go is into the arms of Jesus. He is waiting for you so He can pour out His love over you. He wants to help you overcome all the things that seem impossible in your life right now and, believe me, He will fight for you.

So, cling to Him. Cling to what is good. Church is good. Reading the Bible is good. Prayer is good. Connecting with other believers in the beautiful body of Christ is good. These are the things that will keep us structured and consistent in our walk of faith. We don't have to stand alone. We are all on this journey together, seeking Christ, and boy is it going to be worth it!

I'm just a girl who was lost. But I found Jesus, and I'll never be the same again. I am no longer who I once was because the power of Jesus working in my life has transformed me from the inside out. Yet God is still writing my story, and I know there's more that He wants to do in and with my life. My hope is that my story, painful as it is, can encourage you that God has a purpose for your life, too. I pray the struggles I've had to overcome give you faith to hold onto in the midst of yours, and perhaps even bring life to areas you feel may have died. I know it may seem like God is distant, or life isn't working out as planned, but you can place your trust in this: God is real, and He loves you in a way that no earthly person could ever measure up to. God didn't lay down His life for you so that you would be bound by your sin and shame. No, He is the way, the truth, and the life, and when we trust in Him and surrender every part of our lives to Him, only then can we truly begin again.

ACKNOWLEDGMENTS

To my husband Marlon. Thank you for coming home so many times to take care of our son and sneak him away so I could finish a call or do some more writing.

To my stepdaughter Ellah. You encourage me that I am a great writer. I want you to know you can do anything you set your mind to, big or small.

To Leo. You are my warrior baby. I know, son, you will do mighty things for the Lord.

To my dad. Thank you for creating a safe place for me to be able to share my struggles with you. You have trusted me, prayed for me, and reminded me always that it's my faith in Christ that strengthens me.

To my family: Aunt Beth and Uncle Steve, Grandpa Shaw, my late stepdad, my sister Samantha Robinson, Aunt Lori, and Grandma Kelley. Thank you for believing in me. Your support means everything to me and has given me the encouragement to keep writing and to keep sharing.

To my church family at NewLife Ministries: Thank you to everyone who allowed me to become who I was created to be in

Christ: Shae, Twin, Kemar, Debbie Lewis (I will always remember you in my heart), Debbie & Jim Peoples, and Ben (and more). A special thank you to my pastors, Tim & Ameka Willard—you not only have been my pastors but my friends. Thank you for your time, your prayers, your covering, your wisdom, your patience, and most importantly your love.

Thank you to Author School for helping me to put words on a page and begin telling my story. I'm forever grateful for the divine connections, the meetings, the conversations, and the precious friends who prayed with me weekly as I pressed past the emotions that surfaced, the obstacles I faced, and the warfare that had to be fought.

I also want to thank **Anya McKee and the team at Torn Curtain Publishing.** I am deeply honored and blessed to have had your prayers covering this book from beginning to end. I would not have this achievement if it wasn't for you.

ABOUT THE AUTHOR

Syprina Quiroz first encountered the presence of God in her home state of Arkansas. As a child she loved being outdoors, fishing off the banks of the river, climbing trees and walking in the forest. Later in life, she would often sit by one of Arkansas's beautiful lakes and stare at the water after a hard day, knowing that it was God who had created it all.

Today Syprina lives in Missouri where she loves to explore the parks and walking tracks that weave their way through her city. In the uninterrupted moments of life, she can be found sitting with a cup of coffee in her hand, reading her Bible and journaling her thoughts.

Syprina has a passion for people to truly know that Jesus is real and is close to us all. She loves opening her home to church members who need a place to fellowship and unpack the journey of life together. In the summer of 2021, with a six-month-old baby, Syprina began her studies in Biblical Theology. Her desire is to establish a nonprofit organization where people who are in need of recovery can find help and learn to start over.

Syprina can be contacted for speaking and other enquiries at:

syprinaquiroz@gmail.com

www.ingramcontent.com/pod-product-compliance
Lightning Source LLC
Chambersburg PA
CBHW030259010526
44107CB00053B/1765